D1408139

The
Learning
Alliance

Robert O. Brinkerhoff

Stephen J. Gill

The
Learning
Alliance

Systems Thinking

in

Human Resource Development

Jossey-Bass Publishers · San Francisco

Substantial discounts on bulk quantities of Jossey-Bass books are available to corporations, professional associations, and other organizations. For details and discount information, contact the special sales department at Jossey-Bass Inc., Publishers. (415) 433-1740; Fax (415) 433-0499.

Manufactured in the United States of America. Nearly all Jossey-Bass books and jackets are printed on recycled paper that contains at least 50 percent recycled waste, including 10 percent postconsumer waste. Many of our materials are also printed with either soy- or vegetable-based ink; during the printing process these inks emit fewer volatile organic compounds (VOCs) than petroleum-based inks. VOCs contribute to the formation of smog.

Library of Congress Cataloging-in-Publication Data

Brinkerhoff, Robert O.
  The learning alliance : systems thinking in human resource development / Robert O. Brinkerhoff, Stephen J. Gill.
      p.   cm.—(The Jossey-Bass management series)
  Includes bibliographical references and index.
  ISBN 1-55542-711-1
  1. Employees—Training of.   2. Employee training personnel.
I. Gill, Stephen J., date.   II. Title.   III. Series.
HF5549.5.T7B654   1994
658.3'124—dc20   94-11716
                                                                      CIP

FIRST EDITION
HB Printing   10 9 8 7 6 5 4 3 2 1   *Code 9470*

The Jossey-Bass

Management Series

Consulting Editors

Human Resources

Leonard Nadler

Zeace Nadler

Silver Spring, Maryland

Robert O. Brinkerhoff dedicates this book to his parents, Robert Huston and Jeanie Lawrence Brinkerhoff. His respect for their combined seventeen decades of wisdom is surpassed only by his love for them.

Stephen J. Gill dedicates this book to Nanette Gill. She has been a source of love and support to him for twenty-five years.

Contents

Contents

Preface

A revolution is taking place in the development of human resources. The traditional centralized corporate training department, with its catalogs of classes and workshops, is quickly becoming a relic of the past. In its place, a system of employee training and development shaped by a new paradigm for learning is emerging. This paradigm is characterized by a focus on business goals, customer needs, the total organizational system, and continuous improvement.

Many training leaders are still working within the old paradigm. They find themselves saddled with an approach to corporate training that is essentially no different from the public school classroom of a hundred years ago. Pupils in rows of straight-backed wooden desks on scuffed wooden floors have simply been replaced by employees at laminate-topped tables in mauve-carpeted, high-tech conference centers. Instructors may use more interaction and more audio and video equipment than in years past, but the technology of learning proceeds virtually unchanged. Large classrooms of employees still sit for long (and expensive) hours of instruction that cover topics someone else has decided these employees need to learn. Corporate training catalogs list dozens, if not hundreds, of such courses. These courses represent a huge and largely untrackable investment, guided mostly by faith and tradition.

Top-level executives who have ordained massive changes in other parts of their organizations would be shocked at the truth of their HRD practices. First, the costs that are typically reported to them for training are grossly understated, the actual costs are two to ten times greater. Second, the impact of common training practices is shockingly small. A training department that sees as much as 50 percent of its efforts translated into impact on the workplace is a rarity; the norm is closer to 80 percent wasted effort (Baldwin and Ford, 1988; Broad and Newstrom, 1992). And third, the cost of not adequately training employees while expecting them to think and behave differently than they have before is eating away at profit margins and leading some companies to downsizing and even bankruptcy.

In those organizations whose training leaders have accepted the paradigm shift, HRD practices are very different. The responsibility for developing employees and directing their learning on the job has shifted to each employee's direct supervisor. Information and skills are provided when and where they are needed. The content of training is determined by the internal and external customers of training. Training leaders are performance consultants and designers of learning experiences (classroom and otherwise). Rather than leading training sessions, they are responsible for analyzing performance impediments, designing powerful learning processes, and helping to implement on-demand learning interventions that disrupt workflow only minimally and produce a measurable impact on business performance.

In any revolution, those at the front are few. They are guided by a vision and not deterred by the lack of articulation of this vision into practice. However, HRD practitioners at the leading edge of this revolution know that fundamental change must come soon to the practice of training. Their organizations, desperately in need of new skills and knowledge, cannot afford training that does not work. They know that the old, centralized, corporate training center model no longer serves their needs.

Powerful new training approaches, with "just-in-time" and "just-enough" learning designs, are beginning to emerge and are helping to create a significant competitive advantage for some organizations. Those organizations that have seriously embraced the tenets and approaches of total quality management (TQM) have learned that, by working closely with training customers and using systems analysis and continuous measurement and feedback, it is possible to transform their training operations. They have become consistent producers of highly effective results.

This book is for training leaders who are already beginning to define and implement the new HRD paradigm. It is also for those training leaders who have not yet begun to change but know that they must. By "training leader" we mean not only those professionals who are identified as "trainer" or "training director" but also those managers, human resource executives, consultants, and instructional and performance technologists who want to help organizations achieve sustained competitive advantage through the effective management of human resource development. Readers who have made the paradigm shift and are applying a new approach to their work will find ideas and tools for maximizing effectiveness. Readers who have not yet begun to change their approach to human performance will find reasons, examples, methods, and suggestions that support them in beginning to break down old paradigms and apply powerful new technologies to organizations.

The ideas and most of the examples contained in this book are based on our experience (approximately twenty years each) as training and evaluation professionals, including our work with dozens of major agencies and companies in the United States and around the world, such as Ford Motor Company, General Motors, the World Bank, the U.S. Postal Service, Apple Computer, and AT&T. We have assisted these clients in forming partnerships between managers and training professionals to design new learning processes that have yielded greatly increased business results.

The book, however, represents a fundamental change in our thinking about and approach to human performance problems. This change has occurred for us over the past five years. Prior to that time we, like other authors and training and evaluation experts, had sought to enhance training effectiveness by focusing improvement efforts on the training program or specific learning event—a course, workshop, seminar, videotape, audiotape, computer-based program, or other educational technology.

Virtually all the major books and articles on training published in the past ten years have been based on a conceptualization of training as a discrete event, largely independent of and distinct from the other business and support operations within the organization. One notable exception to this literature is Gloria Gery's book, *Electronic Performance Support Systems.* Gery's concept of immediate, on-line learning support operationalizes a new view of training (Gery, 1991). But even the comprehensive approaches that strive for greater results from training are based on a paradigm of the training program as the causal factor that influences human performance in the workplace. They may suggest that greater impact can be achieved by "bolting on" measurement and analysis activities before and after the training program, but essentially the training event is the locus of learning and change. The very terminology of instructional systems design (ISD) is founded on a belief that discrete training programs can somehow, if they are only more effectively managed, bring about the change that organizations are desperately seeking. Terms such as *front-end analysis, follow-up evaluation,* and *post-training evaluation* perpetuate the view that training programs are the point of leverage for bringing about learning and change in employees.

We now believe that this view of human resource development is a misperception of the factors that actually create significant results for an organization. The approach presented in this book holds that human performance can be improved only when training is viewed and managed as a process within a system that transcends typical organizational and administrative boundaries.

By understanding the laws and principles of systems thinking and their impact on human resource development, we will switch to the new paradigm. The shift in thinking is from departmentalization to interdependence, from program to process, from quick fix to analytic solutions, from short-term results to long-term results, from costly change to leveraged change, and from blaming the system to owning the system.

The new paradigm requires that employee learning be seen not as the job of just the "training department" but that training is *everyone's* business. Only when managers, supervisors, support staff, and trainees, as well as training professionals, collaborate to manage systematically the learning and behavior change process will training consistently and cost-effectively deliver the results needed to build and sustain a competitive advantage.

In *The Learning Alliance,* we present an approach that organizes the principles and processes of the emerging HRD paradigm. We call this approach highly effective training (HET), and we provide clear step-by-step guidelines that training leaders can use to transform training or to improve those efforts they have already begun. Each chapter contains many examples drawn from our experience. In several cases, we describe actual application tools and present guidelines for their use. We believe that the impact mapping tool described in Chapter Four is especially useful.

Organization and Contents

The first chapter contrasts the old training-as-program paradigm with the new systems paradigm. It presents the basic beliefs and values that are the foundation of the new paradigm, explains why these beliefs and values are emerging within the field of human resource development, and introduces a four-part process approach to training that highlights points of leverage for increasing the value added by training.

Chapter Two presents a vision of the highly effective training approach, focusing particularly on the new roles that training leaders and others in organizations must play. We recognize that the shift to the new paradigm calls for fundamental and dramatic changes in training beliefs and practices. This chapter shows how training leaders and nontraining personnel must work in close alliance to increase the value added by training. Real-life examples illustrate the potentially difficult changes that all parties in the training process must make to facilitate the transition to the HET approach.

Chapter Three discusses the myths that have shaped the old training paradigm and still influence many organizations today. Each myth is defined and then illustrated with examples. Readers will be able to diagnose similar thinking in their own organizations that has the effect of undermining achievement of strategic goals.

Chapter Four presents an operational framework for escaping the myths of the old paradigm. The chapter describes a tool called the impact map, which we have used effectively in planning and implementing highly effective training in a variety of organizational settings. The impact mapping technique is valuable because it clearly and graphically depicts the complex linkage of training with trainee learning, trainee performance, and the organization's strategic goals. The map enables all stakeholders in the training process to visualize and understand their roles so that training can be used to add value to the organization.

Chapter Five provides an analysis of the approach to highly effective training, represented in part by the impact map, and shows how this approach is driven by four basic principles that follow from the new HRD paradigm:

1. Strengthen the linkage of training results to critical business goals
2. Maintain a strong customer service focus
3. Integrate training efforts into a total performance improvement system
4. Use measurement and feedback to continuously improve the process of learning and change

By applying these principles in their organizations, training leaders can make the transition to the new approach to changing human performance.

Chapters Six through Nine examine the four principles in greater depth. These four chapters present guidelines to help readers apply each principle, and they contain a variety of examples from our work and the work of others that show how the principles have been applied in the past.

Finally, Chapter Ten reviews strategies for implementing HET and includes a checklist for guiding the work of training leaders. The checklist organizes actions according to the four HET subprocesses and the four principles of the new approach, in effect outlining the key concepts and strategies described throughout the book.

June 1994   Robert O. Brinkerhoff
Kalamazoo, Michigan

Stephen J. Gill
Ann Arbor, Michigan

The Authors

Robert O. Brinkerhoff is professor of educational leadership in the College of Education at Western Michigan University. He came there in 1978 from the University of Virginia, where he was a faculty member specializing in program evaluation. He was associate director of the Evaluation Center at Western Michigan University until 1983, when he joined the Educational Leadership Department to formulate a new graduate concentration in human resource development.

Brinkerhoff's career in HRD began in 1964, when he was commissioned as an officer in the United States Navy and served in a variety of training leadership roles until 1969. During a Post-Vietnam-era sabbatical, he conducted sailing charters throughout the Caribbean, where he also worked on a fishing boat and managed a car rental agency on the island of Barbados. He earned a master's degree in educational psychology in 1971 and a doctorate in program evaluation in 1974, both from the University of Virginia. While a graduate student, he worked as a carpenter and continued his training career, directing the Charlottesville, Virginia, Neighborhood Youth Corps training programs and a number of storefront educational projects for disadvantaged workers and the hardcore unemployed.

From 1975 until 1983 Brinkerhoff directed the Evaluation Training Consortium for the Bureau of Education for the Handicapped. This project was the U.S. Department of Education's largest investment in program evaluation training. The project provided hundreds of training workshops to more than four thousand special education professionals throughout the United States. This project gave Brinkerhoff the opportunity to conduct continuing research on training effectiveness while developing and testing a range of approaches to evaluating the impact of training on organizational performance.

Brinkerhoff has provided consultation on training evaluation and effectiveness to dozens of companies and agencies around the globe. He has conducted training and worked with training leaders in Russia, South Africa, Australia, Europe, the Far East, and extensively throughout the United States. His work on evaluation is used in a multitude of international settings and companies, including Apple Computer, Allstate Insurance Company, General Motors, Anglo-American Corporation, AT&T, and the World Bank. Brinkerhoff is the author of seven books on evaluation and training, including *Achieving Results From Training* (1987), *Practical Productivity Measurement* (1988), and *Evaluating Training in Business and Industry* (1989). He lives in Richland, Michigan, with his wife, son, and three daughters.

Stephen J. Gill is an independent consultant based in Ann Arbor, Michigan. He earned a B.A. degree (1969) in psychology from the University of Minnesota and earned both his M.A. degree (1974) in counselor education and his Ph.D. degree (1976) in counseling psychology from Northwestern University. As part of his doctoral studies, he designed the College Student Goals Inventory, which has been used on campuses throughout the United States and in at least four other countries.

Gill taught in the College of Education at the University of Wisconsin, Milwaukee, from 1976 to 1977 and was assistant professor of guidance and counseling in the School of Education of the University of Michigan from 1977 to 1984. During that period he conducted research on training methods, focusing on the use of videotaped models of interviewing behavior to train counselors. He also studied needs analysis and program evaluation methodology. He joined Formative Evaluation Research Associates (FERA) in Ann Arbor in 1984 as a senior consultant and became a principal and part-owner of the consulting group in 1987. As a FERA consultant, Gill conducted many training needs analysis and evaluation studies for social service, government, and business clients. In 1992, Gill joined United Training Services in Southfield, Michigan, as a senior consultant and continued his work with training needs analysis and evaluation for many corporate clients.

Gill is now a consultant for human resource development, providing training needs analysis and program evaluation services. His clients have included General Motors, Chrysler Corporation, AutoAlliance, Steelcase, Michigan Consolidated Gas Company, Columbia Healthcare, and divisions of the Ford Motor Company.

From 1989 to 1990, Gill was president of the Ann Arbor chapter of the American Society for Training and Development. He also served as program chairperson and in other leadership roles in the chapter during a six-year period. In addition, Gill has written more than thirty articles and book chapters and developed several manuals and handbooks on the program evaluation process.

1

Beyond the Classroom: A Systems Approach to Organizational Learning

This chapter describes the new training paradigm that is emerging in human resource development and presents a practical approach for applying this paradigm. We begin by telling a story about waiting lists as an indicator of training effectiveness. The waiting list notion symbolizes the old paradigm and suggests what is wrong with that way of thinking. After providing examples of how the new paradigm is changing some businesses, we outline the approach to its application. We have called this approach highly effective training (HET). It has four subprocesses:

1. Formulating training goals
2. Planning training strategy
3. Producing learning outcomes
4. Supporting performance improvement

Training leaders, supervisors, managers, and others all have a role to play in performance improvement. These roles are discussed as they are played out in each of the four subprocesses.

The Fallacy of the Waiting List

Several years ago we asked a training director responsible for all corporate training in a Fortune 200 company how things were going.

1

"Great," he replied. "We've got waiting lists for nearly a third of all our courses!" At the time of this conversation, nearly eight years ago, the training director's comment struck us as a singular indicator of worthy achievement. Had the opposite been true, that no one attended the training department's courses, the training director would have been rightfully worried. Who could blame him?

The logic of the training director's thinking was unassailable. To him, his department's job was to provide courses that the organization needed. The fact that there were waiting lists for the courses meant that the department was doing it right and doing it well. Moreover, unit managers, who had to pay for the training courses out of their own budgets (the charge-back system), would not be spending their money and their employees' time on training that did not add value. If courses were not relevant and not useful, they would soon become unpopular and very few employees would enroll in them. Conversely, if courses were needed, they would be popular and the course registers would be full. If courses became oversubscribed, with employees waiting to get in, then clearly the course content was vital to the company. Therefore, a waiting list indicated a "great" program.

Given this mental model, the training director was justifiably pleased with the waiting list phenomenon. He had proof that his courses were in demand. He could reasonably request an increase in his budget for the next year. As long as he had full courses, waiting lists, and busy instructors, all was well in the land of corporate training.

Not until several years later did the fallacy of the waiting list argument crystallize for us the urgent need to change the way we think about corporate training. In fact, the waiting lists meant that there were deep and serious flaws not only in that training department but also in the way the entire company approached training.

Let us assume that the happy training director had analyzed the company's needs and accurately determined that all of the training courses were truly important, that only what was needed was being offered, and that only those people who needed the courses signed up for them. He still could not be sure that the training department was effectively and efficiently delivering training to its customers. The same waiting lists that were evidence of success to the training director could also have been symptoms of problems.

Waiting lists indicate that training is delivered to people well after they can use it. In our example, the training department's customers, those people on the waiting lists, were probably frustrated with what appeared to them to be poor service from the department. Another group of customers, seeing the waiting lists, probably expressed their frustration by looking elsewhere or simply giving up entirely on receiving the training they needed. Even when we give the training department the benefit of the doubt and assume that the trainees were receiving much needed training, the department could not have been serving its customers well.

What if many of the courses were not vital to meeting the company's business needs? What if the registration procedure failed to screen out people for whom the courses would not fulfill their personal or job performance needs? What if some managers sent employees to the training without analyzing performance needs first? What if some people attended, or put themselves on the waiting list, to escape a punishing work environment? What if some of the courses listed in the course catalog were scheduled even though the business need that originally had justified them was no longer valid? What if some employees enrolled in particular courses to qualify for their jobs, but those courses did not result in the transfer of learning to the workplace?

These various scenarios suggest the following possibilities:

> Some employees were receiving the right training, when they needed it.
>
> Some employees were receiving the right training, but too late.
>
> Some employees were waiting for training that they did not need.
>
> Some employees were receiving training that they did not need.
>
> Training leaders had an erroneous perception of the success of their program.

Four of these five possibilities, if true, indicate a tremendous waste of resources. The amount of money squandered in this kind of situation could equal the profit margin of most large and small companies. The single largest expense of training, which is the cost of the time that trainees spend in learning activities, is of no value to the organization.

Recently, we contacted the previously proud training director to find out the status of his department. We learned that his budgets had been cut deeply in each of the past five years, course enrollments were down drastically, the number of courses offered was significantly lower, and staff had been reduced accordingly. The director was concerned that the department might be eliminated. This tale is retold many times as company after company cuts back on its training budget as a way to achieve major cuts in total operating costs.

We have found, sadly enough, very few examples of the right employees receiving the right training when they needed it and then being successful using it. In the vast majority of cases, the scenarios were more like the picture painted above: the wrong employees, the wrong training, at the wrong time, and without the support needed to use what was learned. Often, we have talked to people attending a training program who should not have been attending it because they did not need the training or were in a job that would not give them the opportunity to use it.

Even when we observed that the right people were getting the right training at the right time, there were many other obstacles to effectiveness. Sometimes factors such as a poor program design or an ineffective trainer prevented learning from occurring. More often, trainees learned what they needed to know, but when they returned to their workplace, other forces conspired to prevent them from using their training. These forces are familiar to all training professionals and are the bane of training transfer (applying learning to the workplace). The forces include supervisors who do not support the training, peer pressure to do things the way they have always been done, a fear of failure that keeps trainees from taking the risks necessary to try out their new knowledge and skills, and reward and incentive systems that punish new behaviors.

For example, a gas utility company required all its field service employees to take a course in customer relations because of a new strategic goal of improved customer service. Employees were taught how to be more helpful to gas service customers in their homes. The classes were full, and the participants gave them high ratings. Trainees liked the idea of spending time talking to customers in the home and solving a furnace, hot water, or stove problem. When trainees returned to the job, however, their supervisors told them that they should spend as little time as possible in each home. "This is the way we do it here" was the typical refrain. For the supervisors, the goal was speed, not the quality of each customer contact.

Our observations are consistent with those of other evaluators and researchers. Tannenbaum and Yukl (1992) found that while most trainees enjoyed the training classes they attended and rated them as well organized and effective, follow-up studies showed clearly that effects were short lived. Transfer of learning to the job was low; sometimes less than 5 percent of trainees claimed to have used their training on the job.

The factors that work against training effectiveness waste valuable resources. The numbers are not small. Training budgets are typically 3 to 5 percent of payroll, but the largest portion of the cost is the time that the employee spends in training sessions away from the job. The cost of being away from the job includes the salary of the employee and the loss of productivity while the employee is attending a training event. In profitable companies, employees generate two to ten times their salaries. To calculate the true value of training, we must add at least twice the salary paid during training to the direct cost of training.

The fallacy of the waiting list symbolizes for us the widespread flaws in the way that training has been conceived and managed for the past several decades. We believe that these flaws are deeply embedded in the structure of training programs and in the mental models that guide managers. Plans are laid and decisions made within a paradigm that equates effective human resource development with a large number of training courses that are well attended and highly rated. This paradigm is in conflict with the growing demands on training to make corporations competitive and successful.

The message seems to be clear: something is wrong with the dominant paradigm for training and a new paradigm is needed.

Although the importance and urgency of this need are not widely recognized, promising trends are emerging. Some training professionals and organizations are recognizing the strategic value of training and giving more attention to how they improve the performance of their employees. The thirty-seven members of the American Society for Training and Development (ASTD) Benchmarking Forum have indicated a strong recognition of the strategic business value of training (Kimmerling, 1993).

The Value of Training

The training and development of employees have a strategic value to all companies trying to be successful within the emerging global business environment. The story of Siemens Corporation as reported in *Fortune* ("The Job Drought," 1992) dramatizes this vital role of training. As a large German automobile components manufacturer, Siemens wanted to produce a new, more effective fuel injector. This new product would help the company reposition itself competitively and increase profits. However, production of the fuel injector would require sophisticated new machine tools and manufacturing procedures that adhered to world-class standards. The company's current workforce was old and had only worked on routine assembly tasks. Workers lacked the skills in communication, teamwork, and statistical process control that the new production process would require. Siemens therefore collaborated with a local community college to design and conduct training that gave its workforce the needed skills. As a result, Siemens was able to produce the new fuel injector, sales have climbed 40 percent per year for three years, and the company has doubled the number of workers on the line. Because of the profits generated from the increased sales and the more efficient production, average wages have risen nearly 50 percent.

The Siemens story highlights two important facts. First, training is central to organizational transformation and to sustaining competitive advantage. Second, traditional departmental structures for training cannot meet all the demands for employee learning. Siemens' long-standing training operation was not capable of preparing older workers for new processes. The company had to create alliances outside its training department to accomplish its training goals.

Employee learning must become a central aspect of any company. We must build the capacity of organizations to learn. Chaparral, a successful Texas steel company in the notoriously depressed U.S. steel business, is a dramatic case in point ("Unleash Workers . . . ," 1992). In an energetic attempt to establish profitability and competitive advantage, Chaparral conducted a major reorganization that combined functions that previously were separately administered, such as sales and shipping, into customer-focused processes. The company also introduced a classless structure wherein all employees operate in an egalitarian manner. A key aspect of Chaparral's restructuring has been an intense commitment to employee learning. All workers are cross-trained so that any individual can handle a broad range of jobs, allowing for rapid change and maximum flexibility. Employees are involved in continuous educational activities. They are given bonuses when they master new skills. In 1992, Chaparral reported record-breaking productivity and tremendous savings in most of its operations.

Motorola, recipient of the Malcolm Baldrige National Quality Award, has credited its success in large part to its training efforts. Education at all levels of the company was one of the keys to achieving its quality goals in products and services. Motorola had set six sigma (a parts defect rate of 3.4 parts per million) as its standard for all operations. The company has achieved this goal and now competes successfully with companies around the world.

Profound and rapid change is sweeping global business and industry. Intense global competition, imbalances in wage and production policies among nations, infusion of new technologies, and increasing customer demands for quality at the same time that labor and financial resources are shrinking combine to put unprecedented pressure on organizations to be more efficient and more effective. Virtually no organization can remain the same and expect to survive.

During former times of change, such as World Wars I and II, the Great Depression, the Vietnam War, and the oil embargo, employees could console themselves with the justified belief that the period of crisis would eventually subside into a prolonged period of calm and stability. Today's reality is more aptly described as continuing crisis. The pace of change will not let up. As Peters (1992) has noted, organizations must be redesigned to cope with continuing and seemingly chaotic change. The new organization must be highly flexible, able to deploy new teams of employees in continuously changing configurations as market conditions demand. An excellent summary of economic and social trends affecting training can be found in the series *Training for a Changing Work Force* by Carnevale and others (1992).

If we accept the belief that the capacity of an organization to learn and to provide superior training and education opportunities for its employees is crucial, then the next question is whether the training and development function as practiced in most companies today is adequate for the task. In general, we believe that the answer is no.

We recognize that some organizations are providing exemplary programs and making significant strides toward restructuring their training departments and refocusing the purpose of training. For example, some divisions of Ford Motor Company are moving toward a restructuring of their approach to training by emphasizing what they call the 4Js: just enough, just in time, just the right content, and just the right people. The training department of the U.S. General Accounting Office is reorganizing some of its previously centralized training to a more customer-focused approach. Steelcase, Inc., a major office furniture manufacturer, has developed a long-range plan to bring all its training and development efforts in line with the company's strategic goals. However, these examples are not the rule.

Systemic Change

The kind of highly effective training that the future demands is not likely to come about without profound changes in the systems that interact with and shape the training process. For example, one piece of training folk wisdom holds that a single supervisor can, in a few words or brief actions, undermine the strongest learning experiences of a trainee. The most powerful force for learning in a company is not the training department; it is the organization itself.

The workplace can untrain people far more efficiently than even the best training department can train people.

The training research (Tannenbaum and Yukl, 1992; Baldwin and Ford, 1988; Broad and Newstrom, 1992) quite convincingly supports what many training professionals already know, that much of the training currently going on does not "stick." The typical corporate training program produces only about a 10 to 20 percent return when return is based upon an estimate of the trainees who will actually end up using the training in their jobs. This level of impact is not sufficient. The pace of change and the intensity of competition are such that no organization can afford to waste large amounts of time on training. The low rate of training transfer not only wastes the money and time spent on delivering a specific program, but it means that many cycles of training are needed to achieve anything close to 100 percent impact. A return of 10 to 20 percent in any other phase of business operations would not be tolerated by effective managers.

Ensuring that all the right people participate in the training process is an important part of making training effective. Designing an instructionally sound learning intervention is not enough (Nadler and Nadler, 1989). Suppose we could increase the learning power of a typical training program by raising the rate of mastery of learning objectives from 60 percent to 90 percent. Unless we were assured that (1) the trainees who learned the material were those who needed it most for the company's success and (2) their learning would survive and be nurtured into better job performance, the 50 percent increase in learning would turn out to be barely a blip in the performance of the larger organization. On the other hand, we could be satisfied with the 60 percent learning rate; if we could get more of the right people into the right training and be assured that their learning would be sustained and applied effectively, then the organization would make significant gains.

The factors that prevent training from having maximum impact do not lie, for the most part, within training departments. The problem is larger and more systemic. If anything, training departments are better qualified and more expert in the instructional process and workplace learning than they have ever been. And they have better technology and better information systems than ever. We believe that in most organizations today the capacity of the training function to provide high-quality learning interventions has greatly increased. Many training departments have the instructional technology to deliver solid learning interventions. It is the capacity of the total organization to manage the learning process for maximum value that is in need of attention.

New Paradigm Goals

Acceptance of the new paradigm will result in completion of the following system tasks:

- Translating strategic priorities into training solutions
- Identifying key learning needs of individuals and business functions
- Managing the key contextual factors that affect the training process
- Integrating training technologies with nontraining performance improvement methods (for example, rewards and incentives, supervisory feedback)
- Involving key nontraining partners such as supervisors and managers in the learning process
- Managing postlearning interventions to reinforce application of training on the job
- Embedding learning into the work process so that employees learn while they work
- Measuring the efficiency of the training process to improve results and reduce costs

The systemic inhibitors of effective training are explored in more depth throughout this book. Later chapters provide practical guidance for making the changes needed to deliver effective training. Our experience has taught us that the leverage needed to accomplish truly effective training lies in working with the larger system and outside the learning intervention. Therefore, much of this book describes the points of leverage in the system that training leaders can use.

The new training paradigm is a set of beliefs about the way training is perceived and structured within the organization. These are beliefs about the following:

- The way training goals are established and related to strategic needs
- How training plans and strategy are formulated
- How the nontraining stakeholders in the process are involved
- How learning interventions are designed and delivered
- How learning results are managed so that learning increases and is transformed into added value to products and services

Process Approach to Training

To help us describe training as a process, we use a four-part approach to performance improvement (Brinkerhoff and Gill, 1992). This approach forces us to take a wide-angle view of training. We believe it will help training leaders identify and assess key factors in their organizations that will enable high-leverage change. The approach is used throughout this book to explain the principles of the new paradigm.

A basic assumption of the approach is that the vision for training is always the same: to add value to organizational products and services. According to this view, the end goals of training are not to produce learning, as in new knowledge, skills, and attitudes, for these alone do not benefit the organization. Only when new learning endures and is applied on the job to achieve an objective that is vital to organizational success does training pay back its costs. New learning represents only the capacity for value to be added. If that learning is not nurtured through the postlearning period into improved performance, the training fails.

The process approach to training has four subprocesses that must operate interactively to add value to the organization. These subprocesses are essential to any training effort, large or small, complex or simple, long or short. The specific activities that are planned for a particular training effort are unique to that effort. However, the four critical subprocesses, regardless of the context, always occur to some extent. When they are carried out well and the fit is seamless, training works best. When they are carried out poorly and not integrated, the likelihood of training adding value is greatly diminished. Specific actions within the subprocesses represent the critical leverage points for ensuring maximum results.

Figure 1.1 depicts the process approach to training and its four subprocesses. Following is a brief explanation of each of the subprocesses with examples to illustrate how they are typically applied.

Figure 1.1. The Process Approach to Training.

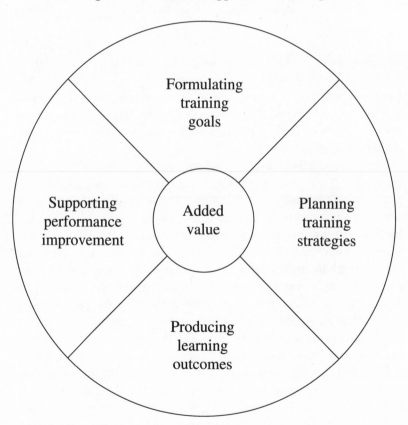

Formulating Training Goals

Goal-setting activities are the explicit and implicit actions that determine what results will be expected from training. In many but not all training situations, training professionals conduct needs analyses to set goals. In a needs analysis, data are collected from customers, top-level managers, supervisors, and the potential trainees regarding the skills, knowledge, and attitudes employees must have to be successful in their work. A needs analysis is a typical goal-formulation activity, but there are others. Another activity involves the planning that occurs when a new machine is installed in a manufacturing plant. The vendor who is providing the machine knows what one must be able to do to operate the machine effectively and safely. Discussion with the vendor about the training requirements for operating the new machine is a goal-setting activity.

When an employee learns about a training workshop from a co-worker and then asks a supervisor for permission to attend, this is a goal-setting activity. The supervisor's decision is a goal-setting activity, too. The supervisor must weigh the costs and benefits of sending the particular employee to the workshop and also determine whether the likely outcomes of attending will help the employee, the work group, and the organization achieve their goals.

The information that shapes training goals can come from a variety of sources. The organization's structure and its strategic objectives imply certain goals, such as improving the quality of products. The way the organization does its business, and therefore its expectations for employee behavior (some call this culture), suggests certain goals, such as teamwork. A supervisor's expectations for individual employee performance define training goals. For example, the norm for word processing in the work area might require that everyone learn Wordperfect. The people that an employee supervises can provide valuable information, such as reporting that the supervisor does not communicate well. Customers of the company are another source for training goals. For example, they might report dissatisfaction with customer service. And, of course, potential trainees are a good source of information; they may have an awareness of their own need to improve performance in a particular area, such as writing.

The activities are not necessarily formal. Any activity that helps people understand what the outcomes of training should be, whether assessed on a test or gathered from a number of interviews with key people in the organization, is a goal-setting activity.

The goal-formulation subprocess may be paid varying amounts of attention depending on the situation, but it cannot be skipped. When training occurs, it does so because someone in the organization has decided that it should occur or at least has not prevented it from occurring. This action or lack of action, regardless of how consciously or conscientiously it was done, shapes expectations for the value that training will add to the organization and specifies the resources that will be allocated to training.

The goal-formulation subprocess answers these questions:

Is there a training problem?
Should we train?
Why should we train?
What training needs are most important to the organization?
What value should training add?

Planning Training Strategy

Strategy planning includes all the decisions and activities that shape the nature and scope of the training process. Designing the training activities, writing training materials, planning workshops, publicizing events, specifying the trainee selection criteria and procedures, getting feedback from supervisors, and soliciting management involvement are typical components of strategy planning.

This subprocess varies in its formality and precision. A senior manager's request for a popular sales negotiation program for next year's sales division meeting, a strategic planning committee's decision after a year of meetings to design a four-day corporate retreat, an instructional developer's selection of a particular workshop module, a training manager's request to have a supervisor involved in the training of a particular employee are all examples of the strategy planning subprocess.

The outcomes of this subprocess are not only the details about the learning events that make up the training process but also plans for what should happen before and after these events. The entire process of training, from preparation of trainees and the organization, to the learning activities, to the follow-up and reinforcement of learning on the job, is specified during strategy formulation.

The strategy planning subprocess answers these questions:

Who should receive training?

When should training be delivered?

How should learning be facilitated and managed?

What should be the training schedule?

How much of the training should be designed before the trainees become involved?

Who should be involved in the planning and designing of training?

How should top management be involved?

Who should deliver the training?

Where will the training take place?

How should trainees be prepared for each activity?

What follow-up activities should occur?

How will the training process be monitored?

How will supervisors be prepared to support the transfer of training to the workplace?

Producing Learning Outcomes

The subprocess of producing learning outcomes includes all of the activities that produce learning. These are the instructor-led, group-led, or self-directed experiences that result in the learning of new skills, increased knowledge, or changed attitudes. The experiences are designed as opposed to being undirected. They are intended to achieve the specified outcomes in the most effective and efficient manner possible. Teaching is certainly a part of this subprocess, but so are other activities, such as managing the learning environment, providing physical and psychological encouragement to learners, monitoring learning, and providing feedback during learning events. If valid training goals have been formulated and the training plans and strategies are appropriate, then the learning transactions can be successful.

The learning outcomes subprocess answers these questions:

Who is learning?
What are they learning?
Who is not learning?
What more do they have to learn?
Is the method a good fit with the learning goal?
What can be done to increase learning effectiveness and efficiency?
Who needs help in learning, and how should they be helped?

Supporting Performance Improvement

Training goals cannot be achieved simply with the trainees' acquisition of learning. For learning to translate into value added to an organization, the learning must endure and be applied over time to enhancing job performance. We recognize that some training is designed for the immediate benefit of employees' psychological well-being, such as workshops on retirement planning. This kind of training is not directly related to adding value.

Where training is intended to be immediately transformed into enhanced job performance, a number of activities must occur to ensure this transfer, such as follow-up assessments of job performance, regular meetings with trainees to encourage the use of their knowledge and skills, and meetings with supervisors to review trainee performance. When training is not intended for immediate use, such as training in emergency procedures for airline pilots, other activities can be more appropriate, such as conducting periodic refresher sessions, providing job aids for use in the workplace, sending written updates of instructional materials to trainees, and reassessing skills and further needs.

We have found this fourth subprocess to be the least defined and planned and the most haphazard of all the subprocesses. Trainers and their departments typically define their role in such a way that once trainees exit a learning event, they are "on their own" and the actual use of the training becomes someone else's responsibility.

The performance support subprocess answers these questions:

What learning can be applied in the workplace?
What value is added to the organization?
How are the new skills, knowledge, and beliefs being used on the job?
What difference does the training make?
Is the value of the training being maintained over a long period of time?

Levers for Maximizing Training Quality

Within the four subprocesses of the HET approach, one can find key levers for maximizing the quality of training. For example, training strategies are frequently driven by concerns for low per-trainee costs. Training is becoming less trainee-specific and increasingly designed for large groups. Instruction is targeted at the lowest-ability person in the group. Invariably, this approach decreases the likelihood of transfer to the job because participants have not been carefully selected and do not have sufficient support from their supervisors.

Some changes in the basic training design can provide strong leverage for increasing the training's level of impact. More individualized training, greater supervisor involvement, small group sessions on an as-needed basis, and individualized follow-up can yield tremendous gains in the number of trainees who actually use their training to improve job performance. After one company instituted some of these activities, the proportion of its employees applying the skills changed from less than 10 percent of trainees to a consistent rate of nearly 100 percent. Although this can be attributed in part to fewer employees being trained at a higher cost per individual, the cost per correct use of the training was dramatically lower, providing a large gain in quality.

Characteristics of Highly Effective Training (HET)

As noted at the beginning of this chapter, we call this new approach to using learning to improve individual and organizational performance highly effective training (HET). HET is simply a convenient name for a set of principles, strategies, tools, and methods we have applied or observed others applying within a wide range of organizations. HET does not employ a series of cookbook-type steps. A lock-step prescription would be neither appropriate nor effective given the diverse circumstances of training in organizations. HET is comprised of guidelines and suggestions for application within a simple conceptual framework that training leaders can use to develop and implement their own performance improvement systems.

The purpose of HET is to conceptualize, design, and implement training as an integrated system that helps organizations use learning to consistently add value to services and products. The key to HET is systems thinking: the assumption that training has an interdependent, dynamic relationship with other business processes and the total organization. This view is in contrast to the prevailing view of training as a separate, secondary function that produces programs and learning that may or may not transfer to the workplace.

Table 1.1 presents a brief overview of the HET approach. In this table, some of the key distinguishing characteristics of HET are shown within each of the four subprocesses of the total training process. These characteristics are compared with parallel characteristics of the traditional, program-driven approach to training.

One of the key messages of Table 1.1 is that training is an organizational function, not just something that is done by trainers or training departments. For training to be highly effective, it must be embraced by all managers as part of their responsibility.

Training creates value for the organization when learning is transformed into performance. A typical training function can only deliver learning experiences, producing only part of what is needed for training to add value. Collaboration among training professionals, managers, supervisors, and trainees is the basis by which HET is designed, delivered, and managed. Within these learning partnerships, accountability for training results is shared by all parties who have a stake in the results of training.

Summary

Many organizations are adopting a new approach to training that creates an alliance among senior executives, training leaders, and

Table 1.1. Comparison of HET and Traditional Training.

	Highly Effective Training	Traditional Program-Driven Training
Formulating Training Goals	• Line manager conducts needs analyses • Line manager is customer of training • Customer and training leader agree on goals • Goals are defined as business results • Training leader consults regarding needs analysis and goal setting • Based on measurement of performance • Based on performance systems analysis • Specifies linkage to strategic goals	• Training department conducts needs analyses (if any) • Trainee is customer of training • Training department sets goals • Goals are defined as learning outcomes • Learning needs are typically based on perceived needs • Usually no linkage to strategic goals
Planning Training Strategy	• Includes before-during-after learning process • Agreed on and created by line/training team • Based on process analysis of business procedures • Specifies accountabilities for nontraining personnel (e.g., supervisors, trainees, upper managers) • Provides for "just-in-time" delivery • Specifies prelearning intervention tasks • Specifies postlearning intervention tasks • Specifies measurement milestones • Based on iterative improvement cycles • Incorporates performance support tools and tasks	• Includes during learning processes only • Created by training department with advice of trainees' management • Based on availability of training resources • Specifies accountabilities for trainers only • Rarely provides for "just-in-time" delivery • Rarely specifies prelearning intervention tasks • Specifies measurement (if any) of learning only • Rarely incorporates performance support tools and tasks
Producing Learning Outcomes	• Incorporates "just-enough" content • Provided on or close to job • Includes practice with performance support tools • Includes action planning • Specifies individual performance objectives • Clarifies linkage to strategic goals as part of content	• Typically front-loads content • Delivered in classrooms • Rarely includes practice with performance support tools • Rarely includes action planning • Specifies group learning objectives • Does not clarify linkage to strategic goals as part of content
Supporting Performance Improvement	• Transfer is responsibility of line management • Frequent measurement of progress and impact • Managed by performance support team • Tracks performance system variables • Training leader consults and facilitates	• Transfer is responsibility of trainee • Usually no measurement of progress and impact • Not managed by anyone

trainees and their managers for improved performance. In the old approach to training, responsibility rested solely with an organization's training function. Training programs were planned and delivered efficiently but fell woefully short of transforming learning into more effective performance that would add significant value to an organization's products and services.

The new approach, which we call highly effective training, is based on a systems view of training and structures the training process into four subprocesses: formulating training goals that are tightly linked to organization needs and strategies; planning training strategy so that learning events are delivered at just the right time, to just the right people, in just the right amounts, with sufficient involvement of key nontraining personnel to assure that the training will be effective; producing learning outcomes by providing and managing learning interventions to ensure that trainees acquire sufficient skills and knowledge to perform effectively; and supporting performance improvement at both the individual and organization levels by monitoring retention of learning, nurturing and coaching applications of learning, and providing feedback to trainees and their managers.

When these subprocesses are effectively managed, training adds optimum value to the organization's products and services. Management of the subprocesses is the joint responsibility of training and nontraining personnel, and requires a new way of looking at the role of training leaders. The next chapter explores this new role in more detail.

2

Facilitating the
Learning Process:
New Roles
for Trainers

Highly effective training is managed as a process that integrates learning events into the ongoing operations of the work of the organization. Training leaders need a systems view of organizational performance, and they need to coordinate the efforts of the key stakeholders in the training process.

The very notion of training as something that is organized into programs is a concept that is antithetical to HET. The program concept tends to separate training from the flow of work operations and leads to the mistaken perception that the training process is the same as, and nothing more than, the learning intervention.

HET integrates one or more learning interventions into a more comprehensive training process. The subprocesses that precede and follow learning interventions have tremendous bearing on whether training is truly effective. We emphasize throughout this book that the larger training process must be defined, clarified, and managed to ensure that employee learning leads to value-added to services and products.

This chapter draws a picture of HET to show what the new paradigm looks like when it guides implementation. The example given here highlights several key features so that readers can have a clear vision of the direction in which the HET approach leads us.

This vision is only a device to provide direction, not a blueprint for delivering training. Nevertheless, we believe such a picture is necessary because it creates an outline, thereby setting parameters, for the detail that is added in later chapters.

An Alliance for Design

In the ideal world of human resource development as envisioned under the new paradigm, there would be no such thing as *training programs*. This term would disappear from the vocabulary of training leaders and all other personnel. Learning events would be built into and integrated with the normal procedures and everyday operations of every job in the organization.

A central part of the vision of the new training function is the role of the training leader. We intentionally introduce the term *training leader* to accentuate this new role and avoid referring to the training professional as a trainer. The role of the training leader in HET is to use his or her training expertise to assist management in achieving the greatest possible return for the company's training investment.

A critical function of this new role involves consulting with line managers and other stakeholders on training needs and issues as opposed to merely designing and delivering specific learning interventions. Although design is a key part of the training leader role, it has a different connotation in HET. Here, design is an important aspect of internal consulting with stakeholders. In HET, design functions at two levels. First and foremost, there is design of the overall training process, from formulating goals to adding value to the organization. Secondarily, there is design of instructional activities (classroom lecture, computer-based activities, on-the-job activities, mentoring, apprenticeship, the use of self-directed workbooks, and so on) that make up the learning interventions.

The larger design role that involves close consultation between line managers and training leaders is a critical and high-leverage activity. It must be based on specific needs and contextual factors. In many cases the learning intervention design function can be contracted to instructional design experts. However, the consultation and training process design role cannot be outsourced. This role requires knowledge of and a commitment to the business of the company and its strategic goals.

Program-Focused Approach

Imagine a company that introduces new products and new applications of those products to its sales organization on a frequent basis and is constantly identifying new customers for these products and applications. In this situation, learning is an ongoing need. If sales representatives are not knowledgeable about the products, if they are not aware of their total product line, if they cannot see opportunities for applying products to customer needs, if they are not able to understand the needs and special interests of new customers, then the business is severely at risk of not achieving its goals.

If we were working within the old paradigm, we would find or create sales training or product training courses that the field reps would leave the field to attend. The training department would be in an ongoing struggle to complete the following tasks successfully:

- Receiving new product information in time to develop training materials and activities prior to product introduction to customers
- Gaining access to product research and development information before it is seen by customers
- Interfacing with the marketing department to ensure that marketing and training materials are consistent in their terminology and descriptions and that training events are sequenced and coordinated with new marketing promotions and trials
- Communicating with field sales managers and field sales reps to clarify sales issues and problems, then translating this information into learning needs
- Examining sales rep performance appraisal data to identify possible learning needs
- Designing training events and receiving the appropriate reviews and sign-offs in time to plan delivery while the training needs are still current
- Seeking an appropriate balance in the training design between competing demands to pack a large amount of information into

one of the rare instances when the sales reps are available and
to keep the content "bare bones" so that trainees can return to
the field quickly and apply what they have learned
- Gaining the cooperation of field sales managers to approve time
  for sales reps to attend training events
- Searching for techniques and incentives to motivate field sales
  managers to support and provide feedback to trainees as they try
  out their training-acquired skills
- Seeking affirmation that the training has provided value beyond
  entertainment and a diversion from the normal pressures of
  selling

Given all of these obstacles and issues that trainers must
overcome in the traditional, centralized, program-driven training
organization, it is little wonder that most of what gets delivered is
not retained and has commensurate value to the organization.

New Roles and Responsibilities

In the HET approach, roles and responsibilities for the training
process would be quite different from those in the program-driven
approach just described. Training functions, such as needs analysis,
design, delivery, and management of postlearning transfer to the
workplace, all require special attention. We can explain these new
roles and responsibilities by referring back to the four subprocesses
described in Chapter One. This approach suggests four major interrelated tasks of the training leader:

1. Formulating training goals that are linked to business needs
2. Planning training strategies that will consistently and efficiently achieve those goals
3. Producing learning outcomes necessary for effective performance
4. Supporting performance improvement that will add value to
   products and services

Returning to our sales training example, we can characterize roles
and responsibilities of training leaders.

Formulating Training Goals

The identification of performance improvement needs and the training needs they spawn is the responsibility of the managers of the sales representatives. The training leader works with these managers to ensure that they understand the strategic goals of the business and to give them the skills and knowledge to assess employee needs. The training leader consults with the managers to assist them in developing an effective performance review process that will continuously identify and define training needs.

For example, the reasons that one sales rep has relatively low sales performance are identified by a district manager in a regular performance review. Through the manager's coaching, along with assistance from the training leader, the particular problems of that employee are translated into performance improvement goals. The manager finds that the sales rep is overwhelmed by the constant introduction of new products, new applications, and new groups of potential customers. The solution to this problem is more complex and systemic than a typical product training program can address. Key stakeholders from sales, marketing, product development, manufacturing, and the training department should be involved.

A committee of these stakeholders is formed and meets regularly to discuss training issues. Using a procedure that the training leader has designed, the committee members review sales data, new product ideas and development, production, and planned marketing efforts. From this review, they specify potential employee performance and learning needs. They consider whether the learning needs can be feasibly addressed by learning interventions or whether other actions, such as alternative marketing strategies and product design modifications, would reduce the complexity of the learning demands. The training leader apprises the group of training feasibility issues and concerns and helps the group sift out specific learning needs. Committee members then create action plans for each of their functional areas to meet the performance improvement needs of the sales force. A typical agenda of the committee contains the following items:

- Review progress of existing training projects.
- Identify and recommend solutions to problems with current training.
- Review field sales performance data and customer reports of product uses.
- Identify emerging performance issues and potential training needs based on new products, applications, and customers.
- Formulate action plans for the next quarter that include new or revised training impact goals; for example, conduct twenty-five application X presentations for product Z for customer group Y in the southeast region that result in twelve product Z orders averaging $2,500 per order.

The purpose of this committee is to project sales training needs far enough ahead so that all the field sales reps will have the knowledge and skills they need to sell new products immediately and effectively, move without delay into emerging markets, and sell new applications for existing products as soon as such applications become known. Members are empowered to act on behalf of their respective functional areas and to commit resources to address the committee's purposes. Their work is translated into performance improvement goals for individuals and functional areas.

Planning Training Strategy

In general, training strategies should provide effective and efficient learning as close as possible to when and where the learning is needed for performance. Strategies should also integrate the learning events into job procedures so that time-in-learning detracts minimally from time-on-job tasks.

To convey new product information, the marketing department gives sales reps diskettes for their laptop computers several weeks prior to new product launches. The training leader has helped design the content of the diskettes. Each diskette is self-instructional, using a "hypertext" format and self-quizzing to test knowledge. The sales reps also receive CD-ROM discs that show an example of a sales rep making a new product presentation. The discs come with quizzes and other interactive query techniques.

Sales reps are encouraged to use the discs just prior to sales presentations.

To learn about new applications, the training leader works with sales managers to analyze new product application trends. Then the training leader translates these applications into a one-page job aid. Job aids are sent to the sales reps each week, along with a reminder to call the corporate office or their supervisor with any questions or concerns.

To prepare for meeting the needs of new customer groups, the training leader organizes customer orientation workshops, which are conducted during the evening in each sales district. The format and content of the workshops have been designed by the training leader. Each session is facilitated by the district sales manager, who has been trained for this specific task by the training department. The manager has been trained in skills such as leading a group discussion, summarizing information, clarifying issues, and asking questions. The workshops include a panel of customers selected by the training leader and sales manager. The design of the workshop allows sales reps to learn firsthand about the needs and interests of customers by asking questions and discussing issues with them. Workshops are held as needed in each district and attended by sales reps who have contact with the new customers.

Producing Learning Outcomes

A great variety of interventions aimed at producing learning outcomes are widely used in organizations. All such learning events, however, must be designed and managed so they will reliably and consistently produce the desired outcomes. For the interventions described above, an effort has been made to place the control of implementation in the hands of trainees and their supervisors. For example, in the case of the diskettes for laptop computers, the sales reps determine when and where they will use the instruction. In the case of the customer panels, the training department organizes and arranges sessions but does so with input from the stakeholder committee and the district manager who is hosting the session. Implementation is always driven by the needs of training customers. Events are delivered when and where they are needed.

The training leader is careful to monitor closely all delivery of training. This is accomplished in a number of ways: paper-and-pencil feedback forms completed by participants at the end of training sessions, direct observation of training events, interviews of sales reps and their supervisors regarding the learning interventions, and meetings with external customers to discuss the quality of the sales process. In all these implementation activities, training leaders have minimal involvement in the actual delivery of training, which gives them time to interact with the various training customers.

Supporting Performance Improvement

Training leaders spend most of their time supporting performance improvement, an important part of the training process. As in the needs analysis and implementation tasks, their role is that of organizer and coach. This is because the responsibility for ensuring that new learning is transformed into effective performance lies with management, not the training function. The training leader's role is also to ensure that trainees and their supervisors (and their supervisors' supervisors) understand the critical issues involved in the application of learning to the workplace. All these stakeholders must have the skills to manage the process.

In addition, the training leader is constantly seeking and developing tools, performance-tracking measures, and other techniques to facilitate the application of new learning. These activities include the following:

- Conducting workshops and providing job aids for district managers to give them the awareness, skills, and knowledge they need to ensure that training adds value; sessions are specific to the needs and issues sales managers face and incorporate actual case examples of transfer successes and failures from their own districts; sessions also include problem-solving activities for devising new strategies for increasing the value of training to the organization
- Developing a telephone interview format to gather customer feedback on the effectiveness of sales and marketing activities in meeting customer needs

- Meeting with sales reps over lunch to discuss the value and usefulness of training materials and activities
- Analyzing and interpreting sales performance data to identify training needs and opportunities and to identify districts or customer groups for whom training does not seem to be having the expected impact
- Designing job aids that trainees and their supervisors can use to guide them in applying their new knowledge and skills in the workplace
- Designing new training activities that address specific problems that are encountered by sales reps and their supervisors as the new skills and knowledge begin to be used in the field
- Conducting occasional surveys of training users that identify learning transfer problems, opportunities, and successes
- Meeting with sales managers individually to discuss the results of all of the value-adding activities; these meetings are brief technical assistance sessions for the purpose of solving current problems and identifying emerging needs; in this role the training leader tries to make sure that the training customer is getting value from the training products and services

Putting the New Role to Work

The foregoing example shows how a training leader might ideally work to implement and manage highly effective training. Now we can identify how this approach to training operationalizes the conceptual premises of HET.

Achieving Business Goals. The training in our example is not simply related to sales goals; training is a primary means by which the sales goals of the business are achieved. The company is seeking new customers and new application avenues for existing products as a means to leverage products and keep ahead of its competition. Training activities not only provide the skills and knowledge needed to achieve training goals, but also help achieve strategic objectives. For example, in the process of sales reps collecting data from current customers to help design the training, the sales reps are increasing their contact with customers and making progress toward their goals of understanding new customers and opportunities for new applications.

The committee of representatives from functional areas serves to ensure that training is tightly integrated with business goals and strategies. As a cross-functional group, members can incorporate key resources, expertise, and information from each of their areas. The presence of the training leader in this group helps ensure that business decisions are made with adequate attention to human resource development concerns.

Putting the Training Customer First. Attention to training customers is initially established and then maintained through the function of the stakeholder committee. This group guides training decisions and advises training leaders on solving performance problems. However, the primary mechanism for maintaining a focus on customer needs is frequent contact by the training leader with district sales managers. The training leader spends more time in the sales areas than anywhere else, talking to training customers and learning about their needs and concerns. The training leader spends only minimal time in the delivery of instructional programs. Training design tasks are accomplished in collaboration with sales managers and other training customers.

Each training activity has variable leverage on adding value. For example, conducting workshops usually has lower leverage than designing learning interventions. Meeting with customers to understand how training can help them deal with their critical business issues is a higher-leverage activity than preparing training materials or organizing training delivery. Training professionals who are caught in old paradigm organizations know that most of their time is consumed by just such low-leverage activities as we have mentioned here. They have little time for their customers.

In HET, the training leader is a technical representative for a sophisticated and expensive product: learning and learning interventions. The training leader must understand the customer's business and design effective products and services to strengthen business performance. This is the job of the new-paradigm training leader.

Maintaining a Systems View. The focus of the training and performance support activities in our example is the field sales system, not just the selling process. The cross-functional committee (key stake-holders from sales, marketing, product development, manufacturing, and the training department) was convened after it became clear that the interrelationship of a number of components of the system was critical to the success of training field sales reps. For example, product information must be designed to meet learning standards, distribution of product information must be coordinated with new product availability, and products, their descriptions, and examples of application must be matched with customer needs and requirements. Moreover, sales managers must learn how to use coaching, supervision, motivation, and incentives to support the use of new learning on the job. Only a systems view of these components and their dynamic relationships can maximize the effects of training.

Providing Measurement and Feedback. Activities to collect data and use information to revise and redirect the training process can be found throughout our example. Sales reps collect data about their customers' use of company products. The training leader reviews sales performance data frequently. The stakeholder committee reviews sales progress and training impact data as a regular part of its meeting agenda. Assessments of learning are built into the self-guided instruction, and similar data are collected before and after group learning events. Measuring and tracking process improvement are critical features of all phases of training in this example.

The Training Leader as HET Process Facilitator. Our purpose in presenting the example of an ideal application of HET is to demonstrate that a performance improvement system, from the perspective of the new paradigm, is tightly woven throughout the business operations of an organization. Acceptance of the new paradigm makes it difficult to distinguish between training activities and business activities.

The example also makes clear the changing role that training professionals must play. In the example, the training leader is a consultant to line managers, a facilitator of the overall training process, and a designer of training that is both responsive to customer needs and minimally disruptive of business operations.

Just-in-Time/Just-Enough Strategy

The foregoing example also illustrates the powerful just-in-time/just-enough strategy that is a logical consequence of the new paradigm. This is a strategy for leveraging relatively inexpensive learning interventions to produce dramatic results.

Just-in-Time Training

The just-in-time concept originated with industry and has led to great efficiencies and competitive advantage from the way inventory is managed. Manufacturers had been wasting large sums of money and other resources on stockpiling parts and other supplies. The practice made sense at the time: parts and supplies cost less today than they will tomorrow, and it is less likely that the production process will run out of needed materials. But manufacturers became aware that in the long run this is a more costly practice than ordering only what is needed and having it arrive when it is needed. This just-in-time practice results in large savings from reduced storage space, less materials handling, less damage to materials, and higher-quality products. The time and cost savings from reduced inventory and handling can be reinvested in other quality improvements. The practice forces people to examine the quality of the processes of purchasing, transporting, receiving, storing, and delivering parts and materials within the company.

In the same way, we can apply the just-in-time concept to the training process. People learn best when they can quickly apply what they have just learned. The "teachable moment," the time when the learning opportunity is optimal, usually occurs as one encounters a problem or situation where the learning is immediately helpful in the accomplishment of a meaningful goal. A time lag after learning increases the likelihood that the knowledge and skills will be forgotten. Knowledge and skills provided after they are needed may be wasted or, worse, allow ineffective or counterproductive learning to occur, resulting in poor job performance and making any training in the particular subject very difficult. Further, a training department that is known to provide training at the wrong time will be held in low regard by its customers.

Nevertheless, training is rarely delivered at just the right time for each trainee to achieve optimum job performance. Training schedules often preclude just-in-time training. Long-term schedules are a compromise that typically assure that nobody receives training at the optimum time. The problem is that training schedules are determined not by what will best serve the needs of customers but rather by what fits within all the organizational demands on the training department. It is as if the customer of training is the training staff.

Company orientation programs are notorious examples of this. Often the HR department waits until a critical mass of new employees have been hired and then holds a full-day or longer session for them. They are told everything about the company history, how the company is organized, which managers are responsible for what, policies, benefits, emergency procedures, how to use the phones and E-mail, and how to order supplies. A very new employee has no context for this information, is overwhelmed by the amount of it, and therefore cannot retain very much. An employee who has been with the company a few weeks or more has already acquired misinformation and learned how to use equipment by trial and error and therefore just becomes more confused.

Training that is driven by "program" thinking often provides training too late or too early for most trainees to make best use of their new knowledge and skills in achieving business goals. Training managers will use waiting lists to control the flow of trainees into training programs. Centralized training departments that offer a popular program will allocate slots to line departments. This will allow department managers to send selected employees to the training program. These practices are prime examples of procedures that have been instituted for the administrative convenience of the training department and to be fair. However, the result is that training is fair only to those who deliver the training. It does not meet customer needs or achieve business goals.

Training schedules are usually driven by mistaken notions about the economies of training. For example, employees with an urgent need for particular information and skills to do their jobs have to wait until a class of sufficient size to warrant the cost can be assembled. This practice leads to ineffectiveness and waste rather than creating the efficiency that it is supposed to produce. The cost of employees not doing their jobs at maximum effectiveness or the cost of employees making mistakes usually far outweighs the savings in training costs.

Just-Enough Training

The just-enough concept is closely related to the concept of just-in-time training. Learning is most efficient when the trainee receives enough instruction at the right time to enable effective job performance but not so much instruction that performance is diminished. Training efficiency is achieved in three ways by just-enough training: (1) job tasks are interrupted as little as possible, keeping training costs as low as possible; (2) no extraneous content is learned—to be forgotten through lack of use or to interfere with other essential learning; and (3) learning is focused on a few tasks that can be performed immediately and recognized and supported by supervisors.

However, as in the case of the just-in-time concept, most training flies in the face of the just-enough dictum. The typical corporate training program is designed to ensure that each attendee finds at least some relevant content in the program. As a result, every trainee must sit through varying amounts of irrelevant training to participate in the relevant pieces.

The Strategy and HET

The content of training programs often grows like coral reefs, accumulating topics as they come along, without regard to whether the additions will add value. In HET, we need to dissect existing training programs and for every part ask these questions: Why is this here? How does it add value? Here are some typical responses to these questions:

We already have everyone in Pittsburgh anyway.
It's in the vendor materials that we bought.

The boss thinks it's good stuff.
Someone from R&D said it's important.
Our trainer is an expert on the topic.
Textbooks often refer to this topic.
We have them the whole week, so there's time.
Some people from marketing will be here; they may need it.
Trainees always have fun with that exercise.

Too much content occurs so often that training consumers have developed a mind-set of expectation that is expressed in the comment, "If I get just one idea I can use from this session, it will have been worth it." This often heard lament expresses a sad truth about trainees' beliefs regarding the economy of training: waste is so prevalent that it is considered to be an inevitable cost of the training business. The goal should be that trainees are taught only what they need to be effective; then all the content would be applicable.

The program-driven approach to training necessitates a one-size-fits-all design, in an effort to assure that everyone gets something he or she needs. Conversely, everyone gets many things that he or she does not need. It is little wonder, given this broadly accepted mind-set about training, that trainers have found themselves in a continuing struggle always to justify their budgets and their very presence in the organization.

The HET approach aims to turn this mind-set upside down by means of the just-in-time/just-enough strategy. Accordingly, each learning intervention should contain only the content and activities that will achieve added value. Each intervention should treat the trainee's time as a richly cherished and expensive commodity.

An example from our experience illustrates the benefits received from and the methods used to implement the just-in-time/just-enough strategy. The setting for this example is a very large (more than eight thousand employees) government agency. The agency makes considerable use of computer and systems technology in its work. A systems training unit within a central training department is responsible for all training in systems technology for the agency's professional and support staff. This unit provides, for ex-

ample, a catalog of courses on a range of topics, such as Introduction to Lotus and Advanced Desktop Publishing. Most courses
are about one and a half to two days long. Even though the courses
are offered as frequently as the training staff can afford to schedule
them, there is often a waiting list to get into the most popular ones.

We conducted an evaluation to assess effectiveness of training
for support staff. While the training was perceived as well organized,
entertaining, and highly professional, participants reported that it
had very little impact on their work. Most trainees believed that they
could not use most of what was being taught.

The experience of a high-level secretary illustrates the lament
of many employees and a classic flaw in front-loaded training. This
employee had a pressing need to begin to produce reports for an
overseas client. The reports were supposed to incorporate sophisticated graphics using numerical and narrative spreadsheets. She contacted the training department, which recommended that she take a
two-day course on new spreadsheet software. However, because the
next scheduled class was full, she had to wait six weeks before she
could take the course. She was able to delay most of the report production until then, even though doing so caused problems for her and
her boss. While she felt that the course was well taught, enjoyable,
and interesting, the topic she desperately needed was not addressed
until the end of the second day, leaving no time for practice. At this
point she was tired and frustrated and worried about all the work
piling up on her desk. She had learned to create the kinds of tables
and graphs the client needed, but doing so was very difficult and time
consuming for her. She had not been able to learn the shortcuts that
would have helped her prepare the reports more easily.

The course suffered from being front-loaded. Because it was
designed for a diverse range of users, it covered an equally wide
range of applications. Because the course lasted only two days, application, practice, and individual help were kept to a minimum.
There was something in the course for everyone, but the secretary
did not receive all the instruction and help that she needed.

An approach was designed to help the training department
deal with this problem. A just-in-time/just-enough strategy was
created to help training customers achieve the results that they
wanted. A training staff member was assigned to be a "business
partner" with two targeted departments. This person worked with

the department leadership to understand critical department operations, needs, and issues. Only after these needs and issues were
understood and specific performance objectives (such as decreasing
report production time by 15 percent) were identified would any
training be designed and delivered.

The training staff member met with the department leaders
and assisted them in analyzing their business operations and training needs. Specific performance objectives were set for the two units
with the most pressing client demands. The training department
courses were "exploded" into their many topics and applications.
As specific needs were identified, the piece of a course that matched
each need was transformed into an instructional module that could
be used by a small group or an individual.

Not all the help provided to support staff was training in the
traditional sense of that word. As support staff members and their
bosses identified specific assistance needs, the "business partner"
arranged for or provided the appropriate services. These services
included the following:

> Brief self-instructional modules on specific applications
> Job aids to guide a user through key steps and procedures
> Sample documents annotated to explain how specific appli-
> cations and procedures were used in their production
> Brief (for example, forty-five-minute) training sessions for
> small groups of support staff conducted before work or
> during lunchtime
> Help-line service to respond to questions of users trying out
> new procedures
> Individual assistance from other employees who volunteered
> to become "resident experts" on particular software
> applications

Training activities were often combined for the greatest flexibility and impact. For instance, the resident expert taught a small
group of staff members how to make the best use of job aids and
then invited the staff members to call her if they needed individual
assistance.

The list of training resources grew as new techniques were
suggested and tried. When more typical training materials were

delivered to small groups and individuals, little attention was given to packaging and appearance. "Quick is better than slick" was the motto. The strategy was to meet needs quickly rather than to build an inventory of packaged training programs.

Summary

The old paradigm of training was based on the classroom approach to teaching, which spawned the creation of separate training departments whose job was to design and deliver training programs. This practice led inevitably to separation between learning and job performance and forced training leaders to expend considerable effort trying to reconnect them. The large number of books and articles on such topics as training transfer and training follow-up are indicative of the problems created by the old method. The efforts of training leaders to reconnect training to job performance and business needs are reminiscent of, and equally as ineffective as, the attempt by the automobile industry to overcome low-quality production with expensive warranty programs. The problem in both cases is in the paradigm, and it cannot be solved with symptomatic relief approaches.

HET is a response to a change in the training paradigm. In the HET approach, training is viewed as a process that is significantly larger than merely the design and delivery of learning interventions. HET employs such practices as just-in-time and just-enough training, and involves the creation of alliances between training customers and training leaders to conceptualize and manage training as a value-adding process integrated with other business and job processes. These practices call for new roles. In HET, nontraining personnel (such as trainees, supervisors, and senior managers) take on more responsibilities in needs analysis, training delivery, and support of training-inspired performance; training leaders have less responsibility for learning and instruction and more responsibility for training design, for evaluation, and as training customer liaisons.

In the next chapter we explore the reasons that HET is not yet widespread as we examine the myths of training.

3

Barriers
to Learning:
Training Myths
That Get in the Way

It appears that the beliefs that many trainers hold about how people learn and change within organizations are barriers to highly effective training. Like the superstitions of primitive tribes, some trainers hold onto certain beliefs long after their truth is refuted by the evidence. Understanding these barriers is necessary before they can be overcome and before change in the training field can occur. In this chapter we discuss such beliefs and offer alternative, more productive ways of thinking about training.

Changing to the new and perhaps revolutionary way in which we believe training should be conceptualized and practiced will be slow and difficult, particularly in large traditional organizations. The training approaches that are used in businesses today have decades of history as a foundation. They are rooted in the traditional values of education, particularly instructor-centered, classroom-based learning experiences. Furthermore, most organizations benchmark their training function against other similar organizations with traditional approaches to the education and development of their employees. This has resulted in a perpetuation of one predominant approach to training.

The current approach to training in most organizations, including all education and development activities, has evolved over a long period of time. It is firmly entrenched in administrative structures, bureaucratic relationships, and personal roles and responsibilities. People in organizations consciously and subconsciously resist changes that they think will create more work, more problems, and greater risk to perceptions of their performance and to the permanence of their jobs.

We use the word *myth* to define traditional beliefs about training that grew out of early experiences but that no longer have a foundation in reality. The reason why training practice is largely ineffective today is because it is based on principles that fit the way in which business has been managed in the past, with complex hierarchies, employees managed within disciplines, and responsibility and decision making in the hands of a few senior managers. However, just as pressure is being put on all organizations to change the way they do business, pressure is being put on training to demonstrate effectiveness in achieving a high return on investment. Currently, training gets only about a fifteen- to twenty-cent return on every training dollar spent. This may have been acceptable ten, twenty, or thirty years ago. It is not acceptable today.

In this chapter we first list and then describe what we believe are five major training myths. Discussion of these myths is followed by an analysis of current training practices and beliefs that perpetuate ineffective and inefficient training. Later chapters give detailed guidance for and examples of new practices that can get the training job done with far greater effectiveness and efficiency.

Five Myths About Training

In all the companies in which we have worked, we have seen the results of these myths:

1.   Training makes a difference.
2.   Training's purpose is to achieve learning objectives.
3.   The trainer's purpose is to manage training programs.
4.   Training is training's job.
5.   Trainees should enjoy the training they receive.

Our experience has shown us that the more these myths are believed and practiced, the less likely it is that training will be producing valuable results. Even where other individuals know these myths for what they are—barriers to better practice—people cling to the myths and, consciously or not, exert an influence that maintains training in a mostly ineffective state.

Myth 1. Training Makes a Difference

The myth that training makes a difference is best explored in the context of two stories. We have told these stories elsewhere (Brinkerhoff, 1989) because they dramatically and clearly demonstrate the reality of the first training myth. They come from an actual training evaluation that we conducted. In the evaluation we encountered two trainees, Jan and Michael, whom we selected, among others, as part of a follow-up study of the impact of a sales training program.

Both trainees are sales representatives in a large international business and have the same job in the organization but in different territories and under different district managers (DM). Each trainee attended the same three-day training session, How to Use Targeted Marketing to Increase Sales Profits. We interviewed each of them about three months after the session ended. The purpose of the interviews was to make recommendations for improving the training of sales representatives.

We chose Jan and Michael because they had performed extremely well on an end-of-session test. The test results indicated that they had thoroughly mastered the skills taught during the workshop. As evaluators, we wanted to find out how two especially successful trainees used their new skills. We knew that any difficulties they might have encountered in applying their training on the job would not have been due to a failure to learn the training material.

We interviewed each of the trainees separately. It was immediately apparent that Jan was making good use of his training, while Michael had not used his training at all. We asked them about their reasons for attending the workshop and what happened before and after the session. Here are their stories, summarized from our interviews with them.

Jan's Story. Jan first thought about the topic of the training session six months before it occurred, when his DM, during a regular performance review meeting, mentioned a critical need to increase market share with key accounts. Then the DM sent Jan a brochure describing the session and asked for Jan's reaction. Jan told his DM that he thought the workshop might be useful in helping him learn how to increase market share in his territory. Next, the DM met with the training staff to learn more about the workshop and what would be reasonable expectations for workshop outcomes for Jan. The DM and Jan then agreed to specific posttraining sales objectives for Jan to achieve.

One month before the workshop, the DM arranged a meeting with Jan and the trainer. All three agreed to individualized learning objectives for Jan and an action plan that specified the roles that each would have in helping Jan apply his learning. One of the objectives to which they agreed was a marketing plan for Jan's sales territory.

Jan attended the three-day workshop. On the second night of the workshop, the DM called to discuss Jan's reactions to the program. They talked about what Jan was learning and how he could maximize the investment of his time in the training.

At the end of the session Jan took the skills test on which he achieved a mastery score. As previously agreed, Jan immediately sent a copy of his marketing plan to the DM. A few days later the DM called Jan to discuss the plan. Two weeks after the workshop Jan and the DM met to discuss Jan's first attempts at using the sales call methods that he had learned in the training session. Jan reported great difficulty in applying the methods and appeared very discouraged. The DM agreed to go with Jan to a key account so that Jan could observe the DM conduct a demonstration call on the customer. Immediately after the DM conducted the demonstration call, he and Jan discussed the process and results.

Five weeks after the training session, Jan and the DM conducted three team sales calls, with Jan being responsible for major portions of each call. Afterward, the two of them met to discuss the calls and for Jan to receive coaching from the DM. Then three weeks later the DM observed Jan conduct two calls followed by another debrief and coaching meeting.

Yet another meeting between Jan and the DM occurred four weeks later. At that time Jan reported good progress in using the new sales techniques. Six weeks after this meeting, and eighteen weeks after the training session, the DM reviewed the interim sales data, which indicated that Jan had increased market share with three of the five target accounts. The DM sent Jan two tickets to a professional baseball game and a gift certificate for dinner at a popular restaurant near the ballpark.

Four weeks later, and twenty-two weeks after the training session, Jan met with his DM for a formal performance review. The market share data that they reviewed revealed an increasing trend for all key accounts, and the two agreed to expand application of the new sales methods to a new sales area.

Michael's Story. The day before the start of the same three-day training session, Michael was in his office catching up on paperwork. He had set up his schedule so that he would be in the office that whole week to review sales data and bring his records up-to-date. He had been making good progress on the work and was looking forward to leaving the office early on Friday to take his daughter and some of her friends to watch her favorite professional basketball team play an important game. Friday would be his daughter's birthday, and Michael had promised her a special outing because he had been out of town on her last birthday.

Michael received a phone call from his DM. The DM asked him to attend the training session that would begin the next day and run through Friday. At first, Michael resisted agreeing to attend, citing his progress on the sales analysis and record keeping. He did not mention his plans with his daughter. The DM explained that another sales representative was supposed to attend the training session but could not do so because of illness. Because the DM had already paid for one person to attend the workshop, she did not want to waste the money. She added that cooperativeness is a dimension on the performance appraisal form and Michael's performance review was coming up shortly. Michael felt he had no choice and agreed to attend the workshop.

On the following day he arrived at the first session and stayed for all three days, missing his daughter's birthday outing. However, he managed to participate in the workshop and achieve a mastery score on the end-of-session skills test.

At the time of our interviews (six months after the workshop), Michael reported no application of the training content to his work. He believed that his own methods worked fine. He was thinking about looking for a job with a different company but doubted that he could find one that would pay him as much or more than he was currently making.

Leveraging Greater Impact and Value from the Training Event. As these stories make clear, the training affected Jans's job performance in highly desirable and productive ways. Michael's performance, on the other hand, was not positively affected by the training, and, in fact, was probably diminished. Even though each of them attended the same training program and learned the content thoroughly, they differed widely in level of performance.

It was obvious to us that making changes in the training session could not have changed the performance of these two trainees. The experiences that they had before and after the workshop made the difference. Only by changing these before and after experiences can one leverage greater impact and value from the training. The stories of Jan and Michael demonstrate that the value training adds to an organization is a function of not only the learning intervention but also the actions and interactions that precede and follow that event.

The interaction between Jan and his manager prepared Jan to gain maximum value from the workshop (learning intervention). Their interactions after the workshop reinforced Jan's learning and extended and further developed that learning. The experiences before the learning event, during the learning event, and after the learning event can sum to a powerful force for performance change and, as in the case of Jan, can add significant value to the organization.

In Michael's case, there were far fewer interactions with his manager before and after the learning session. The interactions that did occur worked to decrease the value of the training program. In addition, the manager sent subtle messages before and after the workshop that communicated to Michael that the training was not important and that Michael's attitude toward the training was not important. These messages undermined any value that the training event might have had for Michael's work.

The stories of Jan and Michael make very clear the fact that simply providing learning interventions, even when the design is excellent, is not sufficient to add value to the organization. However, when the training process is viewed and managed as a larger, more extensive process that involves the trainee's supervisor, then it can make a positive difference. Unfortunately, training in most organizations is treated as if it were solely the learning event rather than one component in a much larger process.

Myth 2. Training's Purpose Is to Achieve Learning Objectives

Nearly all books and articles about training design go to great lengths to argue that training practitioners should define learning objectives in concrete, clear, measurable terms (for a few examples see Mager, 1984a; Goldstein, 1986; Gagne and Briggs, 1979). This is very good advice for designing the learning intervention. The purpose of the learning intervention, such as a workshop, manual, self-instructional workbook, videotape, or computer-based training, is to produce learning. Having a learning objective furthers this purpose. However, as already explained, learning interventions alone do not necessarily add value to the organization. Learning interventions, and therefore learning objectives, play only a minor part in the larger training story.

Imagine, for example, that the Hardaz Nails Company, faced with growing national and international competition in the building materials business, has decided to gain a competitive advantage by positioning itself as first in customer service. The training department is called on to design a customer service training program. Excited by this opportunity and in the best instructional design tradition, the trainers identify concrete, clear, and measurable objectives for a workshop on customer service and proceed to deliver this workshop to everyone in the company. The workshop receives rave reviews from employees at every level, and participants demonstrate through tests and performance measures that they have achieved the instructional objectives of the course. Has the purpose of training been met? We wish it were that simple. The Hardaz Nails Company fails to increase customer satisfaction after the training program and continues to lose market share.

What has happened? Hardaz Nails rewards its field sales people according to increases in monthly sales figures, rewards its inventory clerks according to number of orders shipped within three days, and rewards order processors according to number of phone orders taken each day. This reward structure is counterproductive with respect to customer service. Employees are rewarded for being fast and for getting products into the hands of customers, not for doing the things that lead to customer satisfaction, such as making sure customers order what they need, receive what they ordered, and are treated with respect during the process. Employees achieved the customer service objectives of the course, but the company's system does not reward employees for applying the new knowledge and skills to their jobs.

The Hardaz Nails training department acts as if the trainee is the only customer of training. In fact, the training department has many customers. Managers of the trainees, other workers who are dependent on the work of the trainees such as inventory clerks, and the end users of the Hardaz Nails product are all customers of training. When these various customers are kept in mind, trainers are more likely to design programs and services for the benefit of the entire organization, not just the learner.

If the learning objective is the purpose of training, then this purpose can be met without enhancing the productivity or achieving any other business goals of the organization. Unfortunately, most human resource development professionals must believe this myth because we estimate that 90 percent of the thirty-billion-dollar training industry is focused on achieving learning objectives, not business objectives. Could it be that twenty-seven billion training dollars are wasted every year?

Myth 3. The Trainer's Purpose Is to Manage Successful Training Programs

The fallacy implicit in the myth that the trainer's purpose is to manage successful training programs lies not in the word *successful* but in the notion of training "programs." The training business today is primarily driven by training in units of programs. Practitioners become certified to lead specific training programs. Companies buy training programs and the licenses to deliver these programs internally. Training vendors sell programs with exquisitely designed notebooks, trainers' guides, audiovisual materials, and even desk gadgets and coffee mugs bearing the program's logo. Corporate training centers schedule a year's worth of programs, disseminating information in catalogs that would put many universities to shame. Every day thousands of employees in thousands of companies around the world attend training programs. Advertisements entice people with $99 offers to teach them how to lead, how to build a team, how to write effectively, how to manage their time, and how to manage stress after just one six-hour program.

The training program has become the center of education and development in companies. It is the vehicle for conveying job information and skills to employees, and it is the product on which the trainers hang their hats. The problem, as we saw with the stories of Jan and Michael, is that the program may or may not make a difference. Worse yet, the factors that determine whether the program will or will not make a difference are beyond the scope of the training program. The training process has come to be seen as the planning, scheduling, and delivering of training programs. As a result, trainers are spending most of their time in the part of the process that has very little to do with whether training will or will not add value to the organization.

Making the program successful, however success is defined, will not ensure added value. In the case of Michael, no change in the training program that he attended would have made him more effective on the job or helped the company achieve its sales objectives.

The administrative and commercial need to put the emphasis on training programs is very destructive to efforts to make training an effective part of any organization. This emphasis creates and extends the erroneous belief that simply processing someone through one of these programs will lead to valuable results.

What is needed instead is a view of training as the total process by which learning adds value to the business. This larger view of training includes activities such as linking learning needs to strategic business objectives, planning management involvement in defining and clarifying learning deficits, planning learning interventions that are integrated with job performance, scheduling learning interventions for high payoff, and creating structures for support of critical activities before and after learning events.

The notion that training occurs totally within the context of a program, like training a wild horse to accept a rider within the confines of a stable, is a fallacy. A structured learning event does not have a separate and unitary existence. That event is one component in a process of learning that is affected by all that comes before the event and all that comes after it in the life of the organization.

Even though Jan and Michael attended the same workshop, they had qualitatively different experiences. They went through the same activities and were exposed to the same instructional methods, but because of their different perceptions, expectations, beliefs, and values—created in part by their experiences with their bosses before the learning event—it was as if two different programs were going on.

To the extent that trainees' performance improvement needs, managerial support, learning expectations, and so forth, are similar when they arrive at a specific learning intervention, the learning event is more likely to be experienced in the same way by everyone. This poses a management challenge to trainers that goes far beyond managing a successful program: managing the training process so that every trainee achieves the objective of adding value to the business. Given this challenge, human resource professionals should be managing a training process and organizational system, not separate workshops and seminars.

Myth 4. Training Is Training's Job

Most companies today have training departments or, as is the case in very small organizations, one or more people whose job is training. This fact attests to the emergence of training as a valued organizational function. Not only are there training (or human resource development) departments, but these units are staffed by training professionals, many of whom have earned graduate degrees from university programs in human resource development or instructional technology and belong to professional associations. This trend has contributed much to the acceptance and recognition of the field. However, a price has been paid for that training department sign on the office door.

The problem is that the name on the door implies that the training department is responsible for learning and behavior change and that learning and behavior change is the exclusive job of the people behind that door. Obversely, learning and behavior change is not the job of anyone who is not part of the training department. The training department has come to be viewed as the locus of all training in the organization. It is thought of as a place where people who have some deficiency in their knowledge or skills or performance are sent to be "fixed." Moreover, sometimes people are sent to this place as a reward and sometimes even as a punishment.

The paradox in this parochial view of training is that 90 percent of the new knowledge, skills, and beliefs that workers need to be successful in their jobs is not learned from professional trainers or educators. This learning occurs on the job, by trial and error, by watching other people in similar jobs, by "instruction" from co-workers, by coaching from supervisors. While training professionals are establishing and protecting their turf, others are knowingly and unknowingly providing most of the training in any organization.

Training cannot be the exclusive responsibility of professional trainers if a company is to be successful in today's competitive environment. Jan's supervisor clearly saw this truth, that everyone in the organization must take responsibility for training. He knew that added value is the result of a process that transcends typical departmental boundaries and divisions.

Many other business functions are breaking out of their discipline turfs and becoming partners in the business of the organization. Quality control, once the province of a few inspectors at the end of the production line, is now attended to by everyone in the manufacturing process, starting at the research and design phase. Customer service, once the province of a few complaint takers at a bank of telephones, is now attended to by everyone in the company who has an internal customer or an external customer. Simultaneous engineering is encouraging manufacturers to stop "throwing it over the wall." This is the phenomenon of an engineering group designing a part in insolation from everyone else and then giving the part to production engineers, who may have to redesign it before it can be made, and so on down the production process, thus building cost, time, and error into the part at each stage. If engineers can break down the professional and bureaucratic walls that separate them, they will improve the process greatly. So too with training. It cannot remain the province of a few professional trainers and at the same time help organizations be competitive and successful.

Effective training happens when line management and others (such as instructional designers, organization development consultants, trainees, and senior managers) create partnerships that integrate efforts in a way that recognizes that training is everybody's business. While centralizing learning intervention expertise can make sense in a complex organization, this should not be confused with thinking that training can only happen in one place or that only professional trainers can do training.

Much of what is wrong with training today stems from a belief in the myth that training is the sole purview of training specialists and a training department. Managers often undo the best training efforts by not supporting trainees' attempts to apply what they have learned to their jobs or by sending the wrong people to a training event. Some managers complain that their workers receive ineffective training that does little more than disrupt their operating schedules. Trainers spend much of their time trying to overcome their bureaucratic separation from the rest of the organization. They use elaborate and expensive needs surveys, focus group interviews, and outreach services to try to hear from the training customers. These are right-intentioned efforts and are necessary countermeasures given the prevailing compartmentalization of the training function. These efforts are sailing into the bureaucratic wind, however. They are piecemeal means of adapting to the larger handicap of administrative and perceptual separation and are doomed to partial success at best until fundamental changes in training are implemented.

Myth 5. Trainees Should Enjoy the Training They Receive

We have no quarrel with the premise that learning is probably more effective when it is enjoyable, and we would certainly not promote training designs that strive to make trainees uncomfortable. However, there seems to be a trend toward training that entertains and pleases the trainee. This trend is a problem because it displaces efforts to make other parts of the training process more effective and it places undue emphasis on the learning event, such as a workshop or retreat.

Several factors contribute to the increasing emphasis on the entertainment value of training. The commercialization of training is one of those factors. Given that worker education is a thirty- to forty-billion-dollar industry, suppliers of training programs are competing for a market share. A major element in selling their products and services is the immediate reaction of trainees to sample materials and activities. This reaction can be influenced by emphasizing attractive materials and entertaining presenters and exercises at the expense of the educational impact of the program.

This emphasis is furthered by Kirkpatrick's model for training evaluation, the model most widely embraced by industrial trainers (Kirkpatrick, 1975). In proposing four levels of evaluation, this model draws primary attention to the trainee's immediate reaction to the event, despite evidence that this reaction does not predict learning, behavior change, or impact on the organization (Tannenbaum and Yukl, 1992).

At the root of the overemphasis on trainee satisfaction with training is the confusion about who is the legitimate customer of training. If training is a service that is intended to help the company achieve its business goals, then senior management ought to be the primary customer of training, and senior managers should be the ones who feel satisfied. Their reactions to training will be shaped by the extent to which training has contributed to business performance and competitive advantage rather than the extent to which it has entertained or pleased groups of trainees. But, of course, it is much easier, and safer politically, to measure trainee attitudes toward the event than to provide upper management with information about how training has contributed to the success of the business.

Into this issue of who is the customer of training steps the ubiquitous, end-of-session survey form widely known as a "smile sheet." Nearly every training session that occurs anywhere in the world ends by having trainees fill out an evaluation instrument to assess their reactions to the training event. While there is certainly value in this, the exercise is quite limited in its usefulness in evaluating the session as a whole. Yet the ease of implementation of this exercise, especially given the wide acceptance of Likert-type scales that suggest more psychometric power than typically exists in the instrument, has led to the proliferation of this measure. Such reliance on the "smile sheet" has created pressure on trainers to obtain ever higher ratings on such forms. To achieve higher ratings, the program must become even more entertaining. This creates a vicious cycle fueled by the focus on the trainee as the primary customer of training. Attention is drawn away from improving those aspects of the training process that could yield greater impact on the organization. And it perpetuates the myth that training is only what happens in the classroom.

How the Myths Impede Effective Training

The five myths are interrelated, and each is a variation on a larger theme: the training function has separated itself from the mainstream activities of the organization. Training has evolved to become an administratively and bureaucratically distanced function. Training staff spend almost all their time planning, scheduling, organizing, and delivering training programs. When they are not involved in these activities, they are shopping for new programs or catching up on the paperwork generated by the workshops and seminars. As a result, training staff spend little time interacting with their management customers. Under these circumstances, only the trainees can be expected to be satisfied with training.

This current state of affairs has produced a system that is not very effective or efficient in adding value to the business. There are simply too many forces and practices working against training for it to have a significant impact. Consider by way of example the genesis and unfolding of a training program (a very typical program) with which we had experience.

Our example took place in a Fortune 100 company and involved a central corporate training department with responsibility for management development and training at all levels in emerging technology. A line manager in a customer service unit approached the training department about a need in her division. She described how mid-level managers were struggling to meet customer demands for enhanced service. The training manager met with the few managers who were experiencing difficulties and eventually narrowed the problem in part to their reluctance and lack of skill in providing negative feedback to their supervisees.

Coincidentally, the training manager had recently heard from a supplier who had offered a program called How to Give Negative Feedback Constructively. The training manager also knew of at least three other units in the company where similar needs and problems existed. A check of managers in these other units revealed enough potential trainees to make a training program economically feasible. Two of the unit managers decided to send all their managers to the session. They reasoned that anyone could use the skills and with everyone going, no one would appear to have been singled out as a weak performer.

The training program was conducted with twenty-four participants. The training director was pleased that she could report this high attendance figure. The trainer delivered a dynamic and engaging session. End-of-session feedback forms were consistent with this observation; everyone liked the training, having only minor complaints about the length of the session (one person wrote that it was "a bit too long") and the relevance of some of the exercises and examples (one person wrote, "not quite like the problems we face").

A follow-up evaluation showed limited application of the content. Only six of the trainees were using their new skills in their work. Twelve trainees reported that they had tried to use the skills but found it hard to concentrate on the methods. They said that they were too busy to really try out something that was difficult to do. The other six trainees said that they had not tried to use the skills at all and probably never would. This training therefore had a transfer rate (the proportion of trainees who used the training in their work with some positive effects) of about 25 percent. In other words, about 75 percent of the training investment would have no return.

Unfortunately, this example is typical, as readers will recognize. Most training does not transfer to the job, and no training provides 100 percent return on investment 100 percent of the time. This situation is a fully predictable result of the approach to training represented by the five myths described earlier. We believe, as readers will see in later chapters, that this low rate of return on investment can be avoided if certain fundamental changes are made in how training is managed and delivered.

The five training myths, which as already noted are deeply rooted in training beliefs and customary approaches to employee learning and behavior change, promote self-defeating practices that fall into four major categories:

- Using misleading accounting models
- Overloading the content
- Not linking training to business goals
- Not building in supervisor support

We can explain each of these practices by examining the training example described above.

Misleading Accounting Model

Most trainers use a misleading accounting model to figure the cost of training. The prevailing method of budgeting is to count, directly or indirectly, the per-trainee costs. According to this model, a training session that has direct costs (such as those for trainers, training space, and materials) of $5,000 is cheaper if it is attended by fifty people than if it is attended by only ten people. In the former case the per-trainee cost is $100 ($5,000 divided by 50), while in the latter case the per-trainee cost is five times greater, or $500 ($5,000 divided by 10).

This accounting model was at work in the foregoing training example. The training coordinator was seeking "enough" trainees to justify the program. However, this model ignores some basic realities. First, the costs of training are increased dramatically for every trainee who attends because time in training is time lost to other work. In most training sessions, the greatest cost factor is the trainees' time, although this cost is rarely calculated.

Another and even more pernicious problem with the typical model is that it ignores the *cost per result* of training. For example, if only six people use training that costs a total of $24,000 to deliver, the cost per result is $4,000. All the people who attended the training sessions but did not apply what they learned to their work still must be paid. That is, training resources are being expended with no results. A far more efficient approach would be to reduce the number of trainees to only those who have a strong need for the knowledge and skills and who are likely to use the training in their work.

The cost-per-trainee method of accounting drives trainers to fill sessions with as many trainees as possible, with no regard to whether or not they will use the experience. This method encourages trainers to work for large, centralized programs. The skill transfer rate will inevitably be quite low. Further, the method makes truly responsive, targeted training less likely. The rewards come from increasing the number of employees who attend the training programs, not from designing the most effective approach to training the employees in the greatest need.

Overloaded Content

The phenomenon of overloaded content is a by-product of the misleading accounting model. The thinking in this case is, Gee, while we're already paying travel and hotel costs for the sales meeting in Pittsburgh, let's get a speaker on the new performance appraisal system, too; it'll be cheaper than putting on a separate session just for performance appraisal. So the session becomes loaded with content, not for sound instructional reasons but for false notions about costs.

We often observe training sessions that are simply too loaded with content. Part of the reason for this front-loading comes from thinking that it will be cheaper to add a little more content because the bulk of the training costs will be expended anyway. Another force that front-loads content is an artifact of the per-trainee drive to add trainees to sessions. This results in a tendency to want to provide at least something for everyone. And, once again, instructional integrity is sacrificed for the numbers. This one-size-fits-all thinking undermines the extent to which training delivers results in proportion to training resources expended.

Another factor that probably drives the front-loading of content is a fatalist attitude among trainers that assumes that most trainees will not learn or use everything that is presented to them. Therefore, to be sure that they get *something* out of the session, it is packed with content. The logic of this holds that if trainees only retain about 10 percent of what is taught, teach more so that the 10 percent will represent a larger amount.

The problem with the front-loading of content is that it assures that very little of the content will be used. When this happens, the cost per result goes up. Worse yet, a training culture of low expectations is created, where most trainees and managers routinely expect that very little will be achieved through training. They value the "getting away" and the recreation, not the opportunity to learn to become more effective. Research on training effectiveness points to the likelihood that training expectations are highly generalized across training programs. Each time people receive training that is only partially relevant, they reduce their expectations for subsequent training, leading to lower effectiveness regardless of relevance.

No Link to Business Goals

The separation of training operations from line and senior management creates a strategic linkage gap that is difficult, if not impossible, to overcome. At best, training is designed and delivered too late to have maximum impact on business performance. At worst, and very common in our experience, the link between training and the business goals is not made explicit. Trainers are not sufficiently aware of how enhanced job performance can help the organization achieve its objectives. Another serious gap occurs when the business strategy is not developed with an understanding of the implications for employee behavior change. When this happens, the business

goals and strategies may pose obstacles that training cannot overcome. If training implications had been considered up front, these
obstacles might have been avoided.

Lack of Supervisor Support

The supervisors of trainees are typically thought of as the enemy.
Trainers believe that they should help trainees learn in spite of their
supervisors: "I can teach them, but whether they use it or not is not
up to me." And supervisors tell employees, "Don't listen to what
they told you in training; I'll show you how we do it here." These
attitudes, as counterproductive as they may be, are an inevitable
result of the separation of training from the other operations of the
company and from deferral of the responsibility for learning and
change to the training department. Both the will and the administrative infrastructure to keep learning specialists and managers in
constant partnership are needed. These groups should be working
together to identify, analyze, and solve human resource performance
problems as they arise and threaten productivity and organizational
success.

Summary

Highly effective training faces a number of obstacles. Most of these
are the result of the way that training is conceptualized, organized,
and managed in today's complex organization. Most training is
driven by accounting and design models that emphasize "programs" as the primary vehicle for training. As a result, training
effects are minimal, and even though trainees may enjoy the training, they most often end up using little if any of it.

Training is usually viewed very narrowly as the process by
which individual learning is produced. This narrow view con-
strains the opportunity for added value and keeps training bureaucratically separated from other business operations. Training is
believed to be solely the responsibility of those whose job is training. However, truly effective training involves a process much
broader than the planning and delivery of learning events. This
larger process must be defined and managed across organizational

divisions for business value to be added. Highly effective training requires a partnership among trainers, trainees, and their supervisors. These partners must recognize the myths that drive traditional training efforts and strive to work effectively to overcome these barriers and make sure that training is strategically linked, responsive to needs, focused on critical content and applications, and supported before and after learning interventions take place.

In the next chapter, we present and explain a particular technology, impact mapping, that has helped us apply HET in a number of settings.

4

Impact Mapping:
Creating a Shared Vision
Among Stakeholders

This chapter continues our effort to make the concepts of HET more concrete. HET is an approach to a complex process: a sequence of value-adding activities that operates to achieve the business goals of the organization. This requires carefully managed involvement on the part of many people. In addition, the learning interventions must be closely integrated with other elements of the overall performance system. In this chapter we introduce a powerful and practical tool for defining and managing all these various roles and activities.

The foundation for success in HET is laid well before any learning interventions take place. It is laid when goals for training are first envisioned and linked to business needs and goals. Then, following this goal setting, training leaders and work group supervisors work together to plan an effective training strategy, deliver reliable learning interventions, and collaborate to support trainees as they strive to adopt new job behaviors. Training leaders, work group supervisors, trainees, and other stakeholders continue to be involved in the training process as they work together to achieve and sustain improved job and organizational performance.

Without a map, these stakeholders will become lost in the complexity of people and activities. This chapter provides that map and at the same time creates a picture of the training process as viewed through new-paradigm lenses.

The Function of Impact Mapping

A prerequisite for the successful management of training is that the process must be clearly understood by all who play a key role in making it successful. If the process is not understood, even the best-intentioned efforts at managing the process will fail. The training process is rarely intelligible to people outside the training department. The process is almost never graphically depicted and communicated to supervisors and managers throughout the organization. It is as if training specialists want to maintain a mystique about their function.

When the training process is explained to stakeholders outside the training function, their commitment and participation are enhanced. Managers who believe that their involvement is critical to gaining a return on their training investment tend to increase their participation. However, this will not happen unless they are told exactly how and why their involvement is needed.

Another reason for communicating the complexities of the training process to nontraining stakeholders is that the very length of the process introduces many opportunities for training to become derailed. As anyone who has conducted training or tried in other ways to improve the performance of people and organizations knows, the forces acting against success are strong. There are many benign but insidious pressures to maintain the status quo, including daily job stress, fear of change, lack of interest, lack of motivation, lack of rewards, and competing priorities. Because of these pressures, people will try, consciously or unconsciously, to disrupt or discredit innovation. The forces that conspire to derail the training process demand that we build a clear and strong vision of where we are headed and how all stakeholders can work together to get us there.

The impact map creates a visual depiction of the training process. This picture highlights the critical roles, interactions, and results needed to achieve performance improvement. In creating an impact map for a particular organization, the stakeholders develop a shared vision of what they want from training. Using such a map helps all key players (needs analysts, instructional designers, training strategists, trainees, supervisors, managers, and senior executives) understand how training can affect the organization and why their roles and responsibilities are necessary to make HET work.

More than any other tool or method, the impact map represents the essence of the new approach to training. The technique requires us to focus on the total system rather than each separate program. The dynamic interrelationships of people, activities, and outcomes are symbolized for all to analyze and understand. And stakeholders can see how training interventions become transformed into value-adding results for the organization.

Impact-Mapping Technique

We begin our description of the technique of impact mapping by examining an actual impact map. While this example may at first appear to be complex, it is, in fact, quite simplified. If it included every customer, every job behavior, every outcome, and every relationship, it would look more like an electrical circuit diagram than a management tool. That level of detail would only be confusing and not useful for communicating with training stakeholders. The aim is to create understanding and solicit involvement, not scare people away.

Every impact map that we have used has been a compromise. We have traded off detailed analysis and an in-depth explanation for basic understanding and a useful awareness. As a concept, impact maps are infinitely detailed analyses that show all the behavioral and cognitive interactions in the entire training process. In use, impact maps are representations of reality, greatly simplified to highlight only the elements needed to gain stakeholder understanding and involvement. The maps should focus on the results of learning and not depict the events that make up what is typically thought of as a training program.

Figure 4.1 shows a typical impact map. To explain this map, we must first explain the training effort upon which it is based. Although we use a fictitious name for the organization, the map is

Figure 4.1. Impact Map Example.

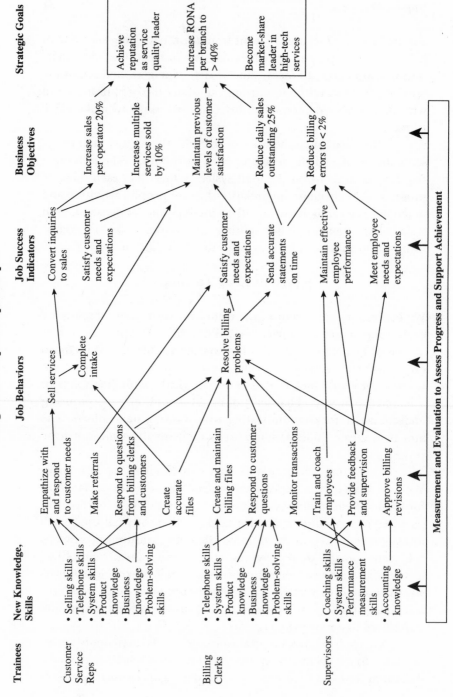

drawn almost exactly as it was used during a training project in a Fortune 200 company.

HomeCare, Inc., a company that provides in-home nursing and other health care services to customers in homes in all fifty states, recently underwent major reorganization. In the old organizational structure, all business functions (such as sales, hiring, scheduling, and service management) were decentralized throughout a nation-wide network of more than three hundred branch offices, with each branch handling all its own business functions. The new organizational structure centralizes the business functions into one office, using a toll-free phone line and sophisticated computer technology to serve customers in much the same way that an airline's central reservation system does. As a result, the branch office staffs were drastically reduced. The newly organized branch offices handle only recruitment of part-time nurses, local marketing, and quality management. Now when a customer calls the locally listed number to inquire about home care services, the call is transferred to the central office. A customer service representative answers the call and, using a computer, quickly accesses the pool of part-time nurses in the caller's local area. The customer service rep, asking questions and listening carefully, leads the caller through a complex protocol and computer screen sequence, and determines the level of care needed, services available, and appropriate insurance options and coverages. If the service rep closes the sale, a nurse is scheduled and automatically notified while a billing record is established.

The new central office is staffed by dozens of recently hired customer service reps, billing clerks, and shift supervisors who manage the operations twenty-four hours a day. HomeCare's overall business goals are to become the national leader in at-home, high-tech health services and to increase return on net assets (RONA) to a profitable per-branch level of 40 percent or more. A business plan specifying call volume, call-to-sales conversion rates, and billing turnaround cycles (daily sales outstanding) has been accepted by management.

The training portrayed in the impact map shown in Figure 4.1 is the training provided to central office customer service representatives, billing clerks, and supervisors. The map shows the major and critical performance steps that have been projected to occur after these trainees have acquired their new skills and knowledge. Starting at the left, the map shows the new knowledge and skills that the trainees are expected to master as a result of the learning intervention, in this case a five-week training program.

In the next column, "Job Behaviors," are the critical tasks that job incumbents are expected to perform as they apply their new knowledge and skills. To the right of these behaviors, in the column "Job Success Indicators," are important and measurable objectives for each job that the preceding job behaviors are intended to produce. In the next column, "Business Objectives," are the specific outcomes the organization needs for business success. Finally, on the far right, in the column "Strategic Goals," are the ultimate purposes of the total performance system.

To demonstrate the connections on the map, we will use problem-solving skills as an example. According to Figure 4.1 problem-solving skills are critical to the role of customer service representatives. The arrows indicate that service reps use these skills to respond to questions from billing clerks and customers and then resolve the customers' billing problems. The service reps rely on help from billing clerks and supervisors to resolve the billing problems. These behaviors are considered successful when they satisfy customer needs and expectations and provide customers with accurate, on-time statements. Following the arrows to the right, we see that successful application of the problem-solving skills eventually results in an important business objective: to reduce daily sales outstanding by 25 percent. Because daily sales outstanding represent services the company has provided but for which it has not been paid, reducing daily sales outstanding leads directly to the company's strategic goal of an increase in return on net assets.

In other words, if billing clerks can receive speedy notification of billing problems as soon as customer service reps first learn of them, billing clerks, supervisors, and service reps can work together to resolve the problems before statements are sent to the customers. For example, suppose that a nurse assigned to a customer arrives late for work one day and the customer questions the time report that the nurse hands her at the end of the day. The two disagree about just how late the nurse actually was, and the customer believes that a reduction in the daily billing amount is in order. The speedy resolution of this issue reduces the probability that the customer will receive an erroneous statement, increasing the likelihood that her payment will be received on time.

For HomeCare, such matters are not trivial. The company's analysis before it went through the reorganization showed that each year several million dollars remained unpaid to the company. Much of this amount was directly attributable to customers' payment delays. Their delays in making initial payments to HomeCare resulted in delays in customers receiving reimbursement from their insurance companies, which led to even more delays in subsequent customer payments to HomeCare. This resulted in large annual tax write-offs for uncollectable debt.

The single line of impact that we have traced through the map shows how the tool clearly and simply depicts the linkage of immediate learning results to strategic goals. If someone were to ask, How do customer service reps learn how to clarify a customer's question? the impact map would provide the answer. That is, service reps learn this skill from their training in problem-solving skills. And because of effective problem-solving skills, they can troubleshoot problems with customers; help billing clerks resolve billing disputes and provide on-time, accurate statements; and ultimately reduce payment delays and make the company more profitable.

With the impact map one is able to trace the chain of events and outcomes that are the result of a learning intervention. The map offers a bird's-eye view of the entire complex process by which specific learning is transformed into benefits to the organization. From this viewpoint, one can see the many places where breakdowns in the process may occur, where the chain of causes and effects may be interrupted and undermine the return on training investment. This helps nontraining personnel see where their involvement and responsibilities have an effect on the value-adding process of training. This understanding is a precondition to obtaining commitment to the support of the entire training process.

We initially used the impact map as a tool to reduce our own ignorance about specific performance systems in organizations and to answer questions such as these about their training:

Why is this training being done?

What are employees supposed to be able to do as a result?

How will this help them do their jobs better?

How will the knowledge and skills being learned help the company?

The map helped us see what we knew and did not know and what questions we needed to ask. Although it had been designed strictly for our own use, we soon discovered that the map is a very enlightening tool for training leaders and business managers as well. Often, these people do not understand the connection of all of the various parts of the systems in which they work. It is very difficult to see the forest when you are standing in front of a tree. We discovered that the map not only helped people see the whole forest but also kept them from getting lost. With this revelation, the impact-mapping technique was born.

Impact Map and HET

The impact map is useful in each of the four subprocesses of the highly effective training approach: goal formulation, strategy planning, production of learning outcomes, and support of performance improvement.

Using the Impact Map for Goal Formulation

An impact map is especially useful in analyzing training and performance needs and establishing clear and measurable training goals that are linked to key business outcomes. If we remove the "Trainees" and "New Knowledge and Skills" columns from the map shown in Figure 4.1, we are left with a map that shows how jobs are designed to achieve important business results. That is, we have a picture of the way the process is supposed to work. Of course, complex organizations rarely behave the way they are designed to behave. Discrepancies between how the job is supposed to contribute to business goals and how it actually contributes indicate a need for training. If we want people and the process to develop in the way suggested by the map, we must attend to these needs.

The impact map is a tool for keeping a clear focus on results. Using the example of HomeCare again, we can measure the proportion of customer inquiries that are actually being converted to sales. Finding a lower than desired ratio, we can bring key stakeholders together and in a problem-solving session track backward to identify where in the behavioral chain a breakdown is occurring. The data from this examination can help managers, supervisors, and other stakeholders become aware of the nature and causes of performance breakdowns. This awareness will help them set meaningful training goals.

Noted below are a number of different ways in which you can use the impact map to set goals consistent with the HET approach:

• Use the map to clarify and confirm the linkage of training goals to business goals. Create a map of the system the way it is currently believed to be operating. Include the desired training outcomes. Then show the map to training customers. Ask them whether you have correctly analyzed the way the current training goals fit into the larger performance system. When training goals are truly linked to important business goals, the map makes immediate sense to the customers and they confirm that there is a good fit. When training program goals are not linked to business needs and objectives, as is often the case, the map makes little sense. The lack of fit will be very clear. You may have to create a linkage when none exists by fabricating potential job behaviors, job results, or business objectives. The training customer will point out how wrong you are, and then you can initiate a discussion about the lack of fit. From there you can move readily to clarifying what the goals should be or eliminating the training, which is a major goal revision in itself.

• Use the map to communicate goals to training customers and other stakeholders. The diagram allows them to understand clearly and quickly how training goals fit with job performance and business objectives. Where there is disagreement, you can use progressive iterations of changes in the map to create consensus regarding goals. HET requires that all stakeholders be clearly informed about goals so that everyone can be pulling in the same direction.

• Use the map to involve key managers in the training process. HET demands that managers play an active and continuing part in training. Often this means taking on more responsibility for training results than they are used to doing under the old training paradigm. The map can help you draw these key stakeholders into goal setting and a sense of commitment to and ownership in the training of their employees.

• Use the map to promote cross-functional interaction. The impact map conveys the cross-functional nature of a business process, highlighting the importance of the contributions of the several different job roles. Consider, in the HomeCare example, the issue of improving the billing process. Evaluation of initial performance indicated a need for customer service reps and billing clerks to spend less time fixing problems and more time meeting customer needs in the first place. This assessment suggested some changes in billing procedures. But changing billing procedures required changes in procedures for customer service reps, changes for supervisors, and changes in form and record design, system software, and so forth. The map helps make clear which stakeholders will be affected by a specific change. Then a new map illustrating the change can be drawn, enabling all stakeholders to see accurately, then discuss, the proposed revisions.

The committee of training stakeholders should continually review emerging iterations of the map to be sure that everyone's understanding of the business processes is up-to-date and that current and proposed training and performance goals are consistent with business needs.

Using the Impact Map for Strategy Planning

The purpose of the strategy planning subprocess is to devise how to apply the most powerful learning interventions—to those people who most need the knowledge and skills—with the least possible disruption to work and business. Because the impact map provides an overview of the performance system and its goals, it is a useful tool for planning training strategy.

The linear nature of the map suggests a chronological order of events, starting at the left with learning interventions and ending at the right with achievement of strategic goals (see Figure 4.1). In reality, learning interventions can and should occur throughout the process. The timing of interventions should be designed to maximize the effects of learning. For example, at HomeCare, supervisors receive some training initially and then receive much more throughout the following six months on the job. Training sessions are conducted every week. These sessions are designed to respond to specific learning needs indicated by problems and opportunities that arise as new procedures are implemented.

The map also has limitations in being able to depict all specific learning outcomes and related learning interventions. For the sake of simplicity, outcomes and interventions are grouped into major categories. For example, the category "telephone skills" represents a set of competencies that includes the ability to operate the telephone equipment, to listen and speak effectively, to make a referral, and to document a call. Typically, this level of detail is part of an instructional design document for a particular set of competencies.

Listed below are the critical questions that training leaders must answer in order to formulate strategy and suggested ways in which the impact map can be used to answer these questions in a way that is consistent with the HET approach:

- Who should be trained? The impact map indicates that all key stakeholders in the performance improvement system should be involved in the training process to some extent, usually as learners but sometimes as information sources or both. If someone has a learning need, then an intervention should be designed for that person.
- When should the training occur? Just-in-time training should be provided whenever possible. Learning interventions to provide knowledge and skills should be scheduled close to the time when trainees will need to use them. The map shows the optimum sequence of job tasks and results. Therefore, this should help in determining when learning interventions will have maximum impact.
- Who should be involved in the design and planning of training? Everyone on the map should be involved. These are the stakeholders who will be most directly affected by the training. We also suggest involving the supervisors of those on the map, for

they, too, are very important stakeholders and will be instrumental in the success of the entire process. The number of stakeholders may preclude including all of them directly, but at a minimum, a credible representative of each of the groups should be involved.

- What follow-up activities should be designed as part of the process? The highly effective training approach is characterized by frequent follow-up of learning interventions to monitor use of the training, help trainees refine their skills, and solve emerging problems by providing performance support. The map can be used to decide where in the task sequence these activities should be scheduled. As training designers review the map to plan follow-up activities, they should look for the following: critical junctures (points at which one task is linked to several other successive tasks), tasks that require cooperation among two or more job roles, tasks that lead directly to critical performance objectives, and other points where performance seems especially important or may be at risk.

- How will supervisors be prepared to support the application of learning? The map shows training designers the specific tasks that supervisors will be expected to support and thus become the focus of supervisor learning interventions. Common among these tasks are providing encouragement to employees and giving performance feedback.

Using the Impact Map to Produce Learning Outcomes

The inquiry and analysis that must be used to develop each version of an impact map are, in themselves, training interventions that can produce learning outcomes. A considerable amount of learning occurs simply by asking questions about how things work. In today's complex and bureaucratically segmented organization, no one person has the "big picture." No one person has an understanding of the entire process by which important business results are produced. Individuals tend to have a narrow view. They focus on the work of their own units and rarely understand fully their interdependence with other functions. The impact map inquiry process provides an opportunity for a dialogue and a flow of information that can help stakeholders learn about processes within their own organizations. This should help with what Rummler and Brache (1991) call "managing the white space," that is, taking a horizontal view of the company and examining the critical people interfaces that do not show up on the organization chart.

Beyond the inquiry process, the map can be a useful tool in producing learning outcomes in other ways, such as clarifying objectives for trainees at the beginning of a learning event. Although it is common practice, telling trainees the learning objectives at the beginning of a session suggests to the trainees that the purpose of training is to achieve those objectives. This is very short-sighted. By using the map, trainees get the long-term view. They see not only what they will learn but also why they are learning. They see the link to job results and to the success of the company.

The map can also be useful in helping work teams (cross-functional and otherwise) take stock of their own behavior. They can look for inhibiting and driving forces. By reviewing the map together, team members can keep focused on the essential aspects of their work and the vital importance of effective teamwork.

Using the Impact Map to Support Performance Improvement

The impact map is a valuable tool for planning and implementing process monitoring and overall evaluation, which are essential for ensuring that the training process does improve performance and add value to the organization. The impact map shown in Figure 4.1 presents measurement and evaluation as a continuous process. Measurement should proceed chronologically, from left to right on the map. First, the extent to which trainees have mastered the skills, knowledge, and attitudes addressed in the learning event are assessed. If the learning objectives were not achieved, additional training may be indicated. Then the use of the new knowledge and skills on the job is measured. This may simply be a check of supervisors and how well they are monitoring performance. As areas for improvement are identified, various problem-solving, revision, and redesign actions are taken. These improvements continue in iterative cycles. Measurement of early events (left side of figure) become routinized as the process matures and stabilizes. Measurement of later events is typically more ad hoc and less formalized.

Initially, the data collection at HomeCare consisted of automatically recording the number of incoming telephone calls that were abandoned by callers who were frustrated by being kept on hold. This measure resulted in a trial solution of coaching customer service representatives to use more aggressive techniques for resolving a request from a customer. To determine whether this new procedure was successful in the early resolution of problems, a member of the training staff interviewed service reps in the cafeteria during their breaks the day after they were coached on the new skills. Because these first informal assessments looked positive, the call-closing technique was continued. Next, supervisors used an observation checklist to listen to reps during calls and to give them immediate feedback. As the technique became routinized and other procedures, such as a peak-hour increase in staffing, were introduced, training leaders turned to the sales system. A measurement process for sales was set up to provide reports on a per-representative basis. These reports gave the ratio of incoming calls to calls converted to sales.

This example shows how the measurement driven by the impact map occurred in iterative cycles, enabling continuous improvement. In this way, the map becomes incrementally more precise, complete, and detailed. As the organization becomes clearer about how the system works, managers gain greater control over processes and higher quality can be achieved.

Creating an Impact Map

In this section we provide steps and guidelines for creating an impact map. These steps and guidelines are not rigid. They must be adapted to specific situations, settings, and people. However, the results should always be the same: a clear understanding, clearly depicted, of the process by which training results are employed in individual jobs to achieve business goals.

The general approach to constructing a map usually involves analysis of documents, such as business plans and job descriptions, and interviews of managers and job incumbents. The major steps in constructing an impact map are listed below.

1. *Specify business results.* Business results are identified for different levels in the organization and should always represent the final output of the particular business function being analyzed. At the level of the whole organization, the results are the overall business goals. At the unit or department level, the results are the unit or department objectives.

2. *Determine the relative order of goals and objectives.* Goals and objectives are ordered in a functional hierarchy such that the progression from unit and department goals to company-wide goals is clear to all. Achieving each goal creates a foundation for achieving the next goal while creating a stronger organization in the process.

3. *Design input-output models for each job.* This means identifying and clarifying the specific and critical resources that someone needs to achieve the desired results and the key outcomes desired from the job. For example, input for a billing clerk might be complete and accurate records of services provided to customers. Output might be accurate billing statements mailed on time and accurate and timely answers to questions about billing statement information and status.

4. *Link key inputs and results to a business operations sequence.* This task requires that the functional dependencies among jobs be described. For example, the map should show that one of the outputs of the customer service representative's job serves as an input to the billing clerk's job. All such critical relationships should be identified.

5. *Clarify how different jobs result in a business outcome.* Usually, unit and department business objectives are achieved because of the output of several different jobs. At HomeCare, customer payments for services received happen as a result of the interaction between the customer service rep and the billing clerk.

6. *Identify trainee learning objectives.* Given what employees need in terms of inputs and what they must achieve in terms of outputs, the knowledge, skills, and attitudes required should

be specified. These become the learning objectives for each part of the process.

7. *Produce a draft map.* The impact map ties together the learning objectives, job results, business objectives and goals, and strategic goals of the organization. A draft map is a first attempt at putting together the pieces of information from the tasks described above. It will be incomplete, having gaps where information is not yet accessible or known.

8. *Review with stakeholders.* The map should be presented to training stakeholders from all levels of the organization. Starting with line workers and moving to top management seems to be the most effective way to do this. Their questions, reactions, corrections, and suggestions are then used to revise the map.

9. *Repeat steps.* A repeating of steps 7 and 8 may be all that is necessary to produce a useful map. In some situations, recycling back through earlier steps several times may be necessary.

The foregoing steps represent the process that we have gone through. The time required to complete them varies widely. Home-Care did not have a final impact map until after more than sixteen months of effort. In other cases, where strategic goals were clear and business operations were more stable and fully developed, maps have been produced in a few hours. Regardless of the length of time it takes, however, the value is as much (maybe more) in discovering new territory with others as it is in completing the map.

Below are some tips and suggestions for creating an impact map. The overarching guideline is to be flexible and prepared to make changes.

* Start rough and increase detail in cycles as you go. Impact map development, like that of HET, is best viewed as an iterative process. The process of producing the map is a learning experience for everyone. A limited start, admittedly incomplete, can be used to provoke discussion that will enable greater specificity and accuracy.

* Keep the map slightly ahead of your current level of certainty. The map works best as a learning device when it increases

everyone's understanding of how things work. As long as there is some conjecture in the map, it will provoke questions and stimulate new understanding.

- Involve stakeholders frequently in review and input. Of course, training customers do not want you to plague them unnecessarily with questions and requests. Yet even if you could create the map by yourself, you would not want to. While a part of the purpose is to help you understand how training is supposed to work, the larger purpose is to build a shared knowledge among stakeholders. This can only be achieved through active involvement.

- Keep ownership of the map with the training customer. The Socratic method is preferred. Socrates, when he taught the slave boy Pythagoras, set out to demonstrate to his friends and critics that Pythagoras already had the knowledge of the unbending relationship between the legs and hypotenuse of a right-angled triangle. Socrates elicited that knowledge from the boy with masterful questioning, but Pythagoras "owned" the knowledge, as evidenced by the naming of the Pythagorean theorem. Likewise, the impact map builder asks questions and records and structures the information collected. The map builder merely draws the map for the training customer.

- Use the stakeholder's language. The map should contain terms and definitions used by and familiar to the people who must use it. This builds understanding and ownership and ensures that a large number of people in the organization can use the map.

- Avoid excessive detail and intricacy. Start with a very simple map and show it to others. Then move to increasing complexity as the customer gets more used to the format and conventions (such as lines connecting results). You can always connect several simple maps to show a complex process rather than try to show everything in one large detailed map.

- Experiment with different formats. The map presented in this chapter represents only one of many possible ways of depicting the links between training and results. You could select other ways of showing these linkages, such as through three-dimensional models, video graphics, or interactive computer graphics. However, choose the medium on the basis of what will work best for the stakeholders, not simply because of an interest in the medium.

Summary

The impact map is a tool for implementing the highly effective training approach. This tool helps training customers conceptualize, plan, design, and manage HET, and its use creates a shared vision of training that fits within the new, emerging paradigm that may become the dominant mental model for training in the organization.

Training should be directly linked to business goals and strategy and delivered in iterative cycles based on measurement, monitoring, and the use of just-in-time scheduling. Content should be limited to just-enough training to impact the next results. Measurement used throughout the training process becomes a tool for continuous improvement, and training customers are directly involved throughout.

The next chapter introduces four basic principles of HET and discusses how training leaders can apply them to make the transition to the new approach to changing human performance.

5

Getting to the Heart of the Business: Principles for Highly Effective Training

In this chapter we define the four principles of the new approach to training:

1. Link training events and outcomes clearly and explicitly to business needs and strategic goals.
2. Maintain a strong customer focus in the design, development, and implementation of all training activities.
3. Manage training with a systems view of performance in the organization.
4. Measure the training process for the purpose of continuous improvement.

While we paint a separate picture of each principle so that its implications can be understood, in application the principles run together like watercolors on paper. In any particular performance improvement situation, one or two of the principles are more strictly adhered to than the others. However, all four principles must be honored all the time. When performance improvement systems are designed according to all four principles, training is highly effective. The principles have been formulated to guide practice and overcome the barriers to effective training discussed in Chapter Three. Greater detail regarding how each principle guides implementation and examples of implementation are provided in Chapters Six through Nine.

Principle 1. Link Training Events and Outcomes Clearly and Explicitly to Business Needs and Strategic Goals

In its most basic form, the "linkage" principle requires that training results be linked to important organizational goals. For example, a company is reorganizing its sales force from geographic territories into product teams. Under the reorganization, different salespeople will make calls on the same accounts but will represent specific products when they make those calls. The strategy is product and team oriented rather than geographic. In this case, a training plan that aims to build teamwork skills would be more tightly linked to business strategy than would a training program on basic selling skills. Although it seems logical to teach selling skills to salespeople, the priority for the company should be building strong teams.

The relationship of intended training outcomes to business goals is critical to the success of training. The value of new skills, knowledge, and attitudes is always relative, determined by the needs of the organization at a particular time. These needs are a function of strategic objectives. To the extent that training goals are compatible with and responsive to strategic needs, training's value increases. When training aims at goals that are not directly related to strategic objectives, the value of training is diminished.

This link between training outcomes and business goals must be perceived by key participants in the training process. Senior management and others who pay for the training either directly or indirectly should perceive the added value. If they do not perceive the linkage, they will not support training activities. Without their support, employees will not be given the opportunities and reinforcement they need to become effective performers.

To create managers' awareness and understanding of the link between training and business goals, training leaders must "sell" their ideas to others. They must communicate the training goals in a way that makes clear the link to business goals and to a payoff for the organization. This will establish the commitment and buy-in needed to further the planning process. As the training process proceeds and other nontraining issues and concerns arise, those involved in training must be continually reminded of its value to the organization. Withdrawal of their support at any time during the planning, designing, delivering, and follow-up of training can be fatal to the process. Continuous efforts to maintain the focus of training on important business needs and goals are necessary.

A performance improvement process can be lengthy and complex. It encompasses a broad range of critical events that start well before learning interventions occur and continue after the initial learning activities have taken place. These critical events are dependent on organization components that typically fall outside of the purview of the training function. These nontraining, administrative domains require cross-functional communication and management involvement. Unless all these stakeholders see a benefit and a clear pathway to that benefit, they will not provide the level of support, involvement, and resource allocation necessary for successful training.

We have found that where there is a clear and shared vision that links training to business goals, training is likely to be effective. This assumes that the organization is clear about its business goals. By asking the questions, training leaders might help management become clear. The answers are easy; it's the questions that are hard.

Conversely, where there is confusion, ambiguity, or disagreement about linkage, training has very little impact. A problem typically encountered in traditional training programs is that trainees and other key participants (such as supervisors) do not see how a particular learning intervention contributes to their work in the long run. The trainees see a short-range set of instructional objectives: for example, being able to use Microsoft Project to plan and manage their product development process. Instructional designers see only the element of the process that they are designing, such as writing a trainer's guide. Training leaders must look beyond these short-range activities and aim at influencing business performance. The training horizon that one should help trainees, their supervisors, managers, trainers, and others to see lies well beyond the immediate instructional objectives. Participants must be shown how, where, and why new learning will be used on the job to impact critical aspects of the business. Even nontechnical programs such as team-building and diversity training, if not clearly linked to business success, will not be supported or have a lasting impact.

The use of tools such as the impact map described in Chapter Four helps describe clear and explicit linkages between training and business goals. This happens when one uses the map as a basis for ironing out disagreements and building commitment before training begins. Then as training processes unroll, one can use other tools to steer and manage events by keeping all stakeholders' efforts focused on important objectives.

In the traditional linear approach to training development, the specification of business-related outcomes, if done at all, occurs only at the beginning of the process, during the needs assessment phase. The HET approach assumes a more comprehensive view of linkage. In this view, linkage occurs throughout the performance improvement process. Trainees can identify job-specific performance factors that are linked to needed job results, job results are linked to unit performance goals, unit goals are linked to division goals, and division goals are linked to company strategic initiatives. Ongoing linkage of training to the strategic planning process itself may be ensured by an organizational structure that brings training leaders and business planners together. In some organizations, training leaders are members of strategic planning groups, and senior managers sit on training and HRD committees and advisory groups.

In Chapter Six, we discuss the myriad ways in which linkage can be established and maintained. This discussion includes examples demonstrating linkage-establishing techniques and concepts within each phase of the training process, from planning to analysis and design to implementation and follow-up.

Principle 2. Maintain a Strong Customer Focus in the Design, Development, and Implementation of All Training Activities

A fundamental premise of the total quality management movement is that quality standards are derived from and measured by customer requirements. After all is said and done, it is the customer's perception of what is "good" that results in the purchase and use of and the level of satisfaction with a product or service. A business can try to influence its customer's choice of criteria for what is "good," but ultimately the customer determines quality.

However, letting the customer define the quality of training is problematic because of training's many customers. Improving quality and implementing effective training become increasingly complicated as training leaders try to identify the different customers of training and disentangle various customers' sometimes poorly articulated and almost always contradictory needs. The typical customers of training described below illustrate this point.

The managers and supervisors of trainees are almost always the primary customers of training. They incur the costs (dollars and time) and they want immediate payback. They are looking to the training to increase the job performance of the people they supervise. In fact, managers do not really want to buy training at all. Rather, they want the results that they hope training will achieve. And they want training results that are low in cost and minimally disruptive to the workplace. Further, and in a deeper but less articulated sense, bosses of trainees often want "painless" results; that is, they do not need or want the disruption that change will entail. Training leaders must help these customers understand and cope with changes in the job environment that often follow from effective training.

Trainees are often seen as the primary customers of training. We disagree with this notion. Their supervisors, and ultimately the consumers of the product or service, are the primary customers. However, we recognize that trainees are customers who have important needs and expectations that training should serve. Trainees have a right to high-quality training. They need training that effectively produces learning results in a manner that maximizes transfer to the job. They may want and expect a number of other features and benefits of training, but it may not be appropriate for training leaders to try to fulfill some of these other expectations. As noted earlier, trainees often expect to be entertained, though they rarely express this overtly. Sometimes they want to be uninvolved and unchallenged and to relate passively to instruction. They expect training to benefit them personally. And they may want the training to take them away from their jobs for a longer period than their boss would like. This is especially true when the training venue is more pleasant than the job venue. Trainers must identify and understand these needs and expectations. Then they must manage them while meeting appropriate needs and serving the primary customers.

Senior managers expect training to return value, to help employees help the business achieve its goals. They also expect training to serve the additional purposes of improving employee attitudes and morale and providing leverage in recruiting and retaining employees. Often senior managers want training to be invisible; they do not want it to cause problems or create resource and time conflicts in which they will have to intervene. Training leaders must collaborate with senior management to demonstrate the value of training. This should build management commitment that can be leveraged into concrete support for the performance improvement process.

Organizational support staff (such as employment administrators, affirmative action officers, attorneys, and accountants) have needs and expectations for training that must also be met, even though they are not direct customers of training. Legal staff, for example, require that training not bias promotion or compensation in such a manner as to create liability. Those involved with hiring and personnel administration require that training activities be consistent with fairness, ethics, and organization policies.

External customers (end users of the company's product or service) have strong expectations and needs related to the training, education, and development of employees, even if not articulated. This is evident in their demands for high-quality products and services. External customers want the results that training provides, but they do not want training to interfere with the fulfillment of their needs and wishes. For example, a bank customer wants high-quality customer service from tellers. But put that same customer in a busy bank teller queue during a harried lunch hour and frustration will build quickly if a teller wearing a "trainee" badge takes a few moments longer than usual with a transaction.

In the short run, training should respond to the needs of internal customers. In the long run, it should add value to the services and products provided to external customers. However, training leaders must keep both internal and external customers in focus at all times if training is to be successful.

Training leaders rely on internal customers for the success of the training process. For example, a trainee's supervisor can provide feedback and coaching that will enable the trainee to refine and master new skills, the trainee can gather performance evaluation data to improve skills, and senior management can create a vision for the organization and clarify training's role in achieving strategic goals.

The energetic and continuing participation of internal customers in the training process depends heavily on the extent to which they believe training serves their needs. If internal customers perceive training as irrelevant, unrealistic, or a barrier to their work objectives, they will not participate fully and may impede training efforts. For these reasons, training leaders must understand their customers' needs and concerns. Training leaders must maintain close contact with these customers to be sure that changing needs and concerns are addressed throughout the training process.

We have often heard line supervisors complain that training people are out of touch with the real work of the business and managers complain that trainers lack an understanding of business realities. Likewise, we have often encountered training leaders who seem to have only a rudimentary knowledge of what their customers need. These trainers are unable to explain the pressures and conditions under which employees have to function. Where this lack of understanding exists, training cannot be effective.

Identifying the customers of training is only part of the second HET principle. Training leaders must also be able to communicate with their various customers. Training leaders should master the skills of listening and understanding so that their customers perceive them as responsive in trying to fulfill customer requirements.

Adherence to this second principle also requires new ways of serving the customers of training, ways that run counter to the instructional systems design approach. Trainers may need to abandon the cherished notion that thorough needs analysis must precede training design. Often, a situation demands that employees acquire new abilities quickly. Limits on time and resources do not allow for a comprehensive study of customer needs. A rapid-cycle approach is necessary, and this presents a trade-off that trainers must make.

They sacrifice initial accuracy in the training content and methods for the opportunity to provide customers with what they want. This does not negate the value of assessing needs, but it does suggest a nonsequential approach to developing training programs.

External customer demands and concerns are the driving force behind business success. To define these requirements, training leaders must know the characteristics of external customers: who they are, what service or product they want; why, where, and when they want it; and how they will use it. Then training leaders must use this information to design a performance improvement system and deliver effective training activities.

External customers also have a role to play in improving training services. For example, customer satisfaction data are used to determine whether training is having the desired impact on trainees. This data can be used to give feedback to job performers, who can then modify their performance to better serve business customers.

Training leaders must adopt a customer service perspective in all aspects of training management. The customer service revolution has had a profound impact on the world business scene and has brought dramatic change and competitive advantage to those companies that have successfully adopted total quality management (TQM). Ford Motor Company, Apple, Xerox, the Body Shop, and American Express are just a few of the many companies that have leveraged the "voice of the customer" into major gains in market share and recognition.

Customer service includes all of an organization's activities that add value to its core business. An automobile repair shop fixes cars. But any experienced mechanic can do this. If all the repair shop did was fix cars, competitors could put the shop out of business in a very short period of time. Auto repair shops, to be competitive, must also provide customer service. The customer of a repair shop wants to be treated courteously as well as to have the car fixed quickly, completely, and reliably and returned in a clean condition. Meeting these criteria raises the level of service and narrows the competition. A shop that can distinguish itself from its competition by providing superior service will win customer loyalty and in the process add value to its core business. The elements of service beyond the actual repair of the car help meet or exceed the customer's expectations. They enable the customer to derive maximum value.

In applying this notion of customer service to performance improvement systems, training leaders must identify their customers, understand customer needs, and then work in ways to maximize the impact of training on fulfilling customer requirements. This principle demands new approaches to training that may be temporarily uncomfortable for training leaders. If a training customer needs to learn a new skill immediately for success on the job today, in-house workshops and community college courses will not meet the need. Alternatives must be found. Full adoption of this principle will have a profound impact on the quality and value of training and will eventually become the norm in performance improvement systems.

Principle 3. Manage Training with a Systems
View of Performance in the Organization

Senge (1990), Deming (1986), and other quality management gurus direct us to think in terms of systems. The systems view is a recognition that elements and actions in organizations are interdependent. A change in one area is preceded by a change in another area and followed by change in yet another area. Fixing or making changes in just one part of a complex system rarely solves a problem or achieves a goal.

For example, a computer service company that is facing increasing demands from its customers to provide more sophisticated and complex assistance in network design and consultation, hires several dozen experienced network engineers who have advanced technical credentials. However, this action will not be sufficient to meet the demands. In addition to hiring these professionals, the company should, at a minimum:

- Revise job descriptions and classifications to enable the company to pay higher compensation to attract and keep the new employees
- Prepare the sales force to negotiate new contracts with clients to include the broader services

- Redesign the contract format to incorporate the new services
- Adjust the billing rates to increase revenues to support the higher wages
- Redesign the billing statement to include the expanded services
- Revise performance appraisal procedures and forms to include new performance requirements and measures
- Adjust merit and bonus procedures to provide incentives for new services
- Inform everyone in the company about the changes
- Orient the newly hired employees to the company
- Train the new employees in the company's way of serving customers

Each of these actions will have immediate and significant reactions from other parts of the organization.

This example illustrates the interrelationship of the various parts of an organization. First, several departments or units within the organization, such as sales training, legal affairs, accounts receivable, and compensation and benefits, must be involved. The contributions of each are needed to make the entire system work. Second, a failure to provide the support needed by any one of these contributors jeopardizes the entire change effort. If the sales training unit does not instruct salespeople in how to sell the new service contracts, the anticipated increase in contracts will not occur and the new network engineers will be frustrated. If higher wages are being paid without an increase in revenue, profits will suffer. Third, and probably most important, all the functions in this example must operate together. They are the components that, when considered together, make up a system. It is the interaction of these parts that makes the system effective. In our example, the purpose of the change (to provide more expert consultation) is not merely to have a highly skilled group of employees but to provide better service to customers. In doing this, the company will become more competitive and therefore more profitable. Attention to this larger purpose helps identify the elements in the system and enables management to bring about a successful change.

All human resource development efforts are interdependent with the elements of the larger system in which they occur. In our example of the computer service company, sales training is necessary to prepare salespeople for selling more inclusive service contracts. Similarly, service managers need training in how to coach employees to achieve the new goals, and billing clerks need training in how to use the new billing format. Almost any organizational intervention or change involves the education, training, and development of employees in at least several, if not all, parts of the company.

The systemic nature of training is evident, as well, from the viewpoint of staff providing the training. The training of service managers in our example prepares them to supervise the work of the new network consultants. The immediate objective of this training is to increase the managers' supervisory skills for working with experienced network engineers. An intermediate goal is that the network engineers provide improved services that effectively meet customer requirements. The long-range goals for this new service are to reposition the company in relation to its competition and to make the company more profitable. In the short run, it is possible for training to be successful in imparting the new learning and behavior change but for some other element of the system to fail, undermining the entire effort. IBM, once considered one of the benchmark companies for HRD, has gone through very turbulent times because of factors related to training but outside the control of the training function. Again, all elements of the system must perform well and be effectively integrated if the system is to be successful.

Managing training from a systems perspective is not easy. It stretches the capacity of many trainers and training managers. However, more importantly, it pushes nontraining personnel to come to new and challenging understandings of their roles and responsibilities in relation to human resource development. Chapter Eight provides examples and suggestions readers can use to implement the systems approach to managing training.

Principle 4. Measure the Training Process for the Purpose of Continuous Improvement

Virtually every book, training program, and speech by the gurus on quality management and customer service stress the key role of measurement in achieving quality results and meeting customer needs.

These experts have found that the process of producing a product or delivering a service is improved when people are able to measure and compare their performance to some standard for that process, such as the number of defects per million parts or the number of complaints per one hundred service calls.

As noted earlier, quality specifications derive from customer requirements. From the initial idea for a new product or service to the final delivery of that product or service to end users, measurement keeps the entire process on track toward achieving the requirements of the customer. Training, as a service intended to achieve quality results, requires continuous measurement to achieve continuous improvement.

Measurement should pervade the training process. Initially, measurement data are needed to identify employee performance deficits and improvement needs. Measurement data are also needed to identify critical activities for before and after a learning intervention; to establish the training objectives; to improve learning events; to assess the acquisition of new skills, knowledge, and attitudes; and to provide feedback on the trainee's mastery of new abilities.

Transitioning to a measurement-based training paradigm is not simply a matter of applying measures within a business-as-usual approach to training. Where we have used a measurement-infused approach, we have found ourselves (and people working with us) working in new ways. Business needs tend to be so urgent and dynamic that training is often initiated with less than the best solutions. These solutions can be modified through an iterative tryout-redesign cycle that is continuously measured. This approach has some distinct advantages: training customers receive highly customized and timely service (albeit a less than elegant instructional design), and a larger impact is more likely, with less at risk in terms of the training investment. Moreover, bad designs are discovered and aborted more quickly, allowing training resources to be put into designs that are more promising.

Using the Principles of HET

The new paradigm calls for training to be guided by all four of the principles described above. Because these principles are interdependent facets of an approach to training, they must be applied in a coordinated way.

Nonetheless, it is typical that one or two principles are not given as much attention as the others in a particular situation. Trade-offs among the principles must be made. In our work we have found that the postintervention supports necessary for peak performance are often not in place. Despite this lack, we have in-itiated small and highly focused demonstration projects, employing a just-in-time training design to address a critical business need. In such instances, we expect only modest success at the cost of consid-erably heroic efforts on the part of a dedicated training team. We know that to solve the problem with more elegant solutions even-tually, we must resolve some portion of the problem immediately. We do this recognizing that not all the tools and information are in place, that we will likely stumble along the way, and that we will celebrate our stumbles as noble efforts and learning opportunities. We do not ignore the principles but simply hold them in partial abeyance until such time as we can arrange the organization's re-sources for maximum impact.

Our advice is to keep the principles in mind all the time. Seek to optimize each principle with respect to available resources. Sep-arately consider and review each principle. If failure to address even one of them adequately will seriously harm the chance for success, do not proceed with the project until a more effective plan can be created. Usually, however, practitioners find that there are interim solutions that pay enough respect to each principle to enable a modest but workable beginning.

Summary

Training leaders wishing to implement the HET approach are en-couraged to follow four key principles in their work: to link train-ing events and outcomes clearly and explicitly to business needs and strategic goals; to maintain a strong customer focus in the design, development, and implementation of all training activities; to man-age training with a systems view of performance in the organiza-tion; and to measure the training process for the purpose of continuous improvement. Training leaders must also help other training stakeholders understand how and why the principles are important. Specific activities within each of the four training sub-processes (formulating training goals, planning training strategy, producing learning outcomes, and supporting performance improvement) should be planned and implemented to optimize the principles. While each training setting poses particular needs and issues, none of the principles should be ignored, though they may receive differential treatment based on particular contextual factors. Each of the following four chapters presents specific guidelines, suggested practices, and illustrations that will help training leaders make the best possible use of the principles.

6

Linking Training
to Business Goals

As explained in Chapter Five, the first principle of highly effective training directs training leaders to forge clear and explicit links with vital business goals and strategic objectives to derive the maximum value from training. This chapter explains the value of these links and provides procedures, guidelines, and suggestions for creating them. Because the HET approach prescribes linkage-building efforts throughout the training process—not just in the "front end" needs analysis activities, where the consideration of linkage typically begins and ends—the chapter suggests procedures for establishing and maintaining linkage throughout the training subprocesses (formulating training goals, planning training strategies, producing learning outcomes, and supporting performance improvement), each of which is characterized by specific needs and opportunities for forging linkages.

Adding Value Through Linkage

The value of training is a function of the contribution that training makes to the business of the organization, whether that business is producing a product, selling a product, or providing a service. Value is determined by the extent to which there is a need for the potential contribution of training. For example, if the effective operation of the core business of the organization depends on the capacity of certain employees to perform key tasks, then training has high value. In 1988, Siemens Corporation, a large manufacturer of auto parts, decided to dedicate an entire factory to the production of a new nonclogging fuel injector ("The Job Drought," 1992). The machinery acquired to build the new injectors was very sophisticated and expensive. It was configured in a new way that speeded up production and enhanced the quality of the parts. The workers in the factory had for years been doing routine assembly tasks. They had no experience or skills in the sorts of statistical analysis, teamwork, and communications needed to operate the new factory. An intensive training program was conducted, and as a result, the new factory was extremely successful and profitable. Workers were producing parts to tolerances that had previously been thought impossible, which led to annual sales increases of 40 percent.

In situations such as Siemens', where the need for training is very high, training executed effectively will yield tremendous value. In other situations, the potential contribution of training may be only marginal because something other than training is needed to make the organization successful. In these situations, even effectively delivered training will have very little value. A health insurance company expected its claims processors to meet certain predefined standards for speed in processing claims. Training to improve accuracy in processing claims was implemented. While of value to the insurance customer, this training had limited value to the organization. This example demonstrates that the value of training is relative. The more closely it is linked to vital business operations and organizational goals, the more value it will yield.

The value of linking training to business goals is also affected by the visibility of this linkage to others in the organization. Particular training results may be critical to business success but not articulated to the people who can support the learning. The potential of training cannot be achieved. For example, an electronics firm developed a new process for improving the quality of products and doing so more quickly and inexpensively. These were the strategic goals of the company. Training was offered to teach employees how to use the new process. However, because managers did not see the direct connection between the training and employees being able to use the new process, relatively few employees took advantage of the training and the process failed to become a part of the company culture.

Enhancing Linkage Throughout the Subprocesses

Linking training to business strategy and goals is often viewed as a one-time function that precedes the design of a new training program. According to this old-paradigm view, training goals are derived from the needs expressed by employees at the front end of the training process. Once this analysis is completed, the training goals are established and the assumption is that little change will occur in these goals throughout the training process.

Conducting a thorough analysis of business strategy and needs early in the training process is a vital function that contributes substantially to the identification and specification of training goals that are important to the organization. When goals are not clearly established at the outset of planning, it is likely that training cannot be linked to business needs. Because it has not been aimed at valued results, training may hit something, but not necessarily the desired target.

However, linkage must continue beyond the initial goal-setting through the total process of performance improvement. Training is a dynamic process that should be modified as training leaders receive feedback on employee needs, on feasibility of training strategies, on effectiveness of programs, and on impact on the organization. Business, too, is dynamic, with changing employees, changing economics, changing customers, and therefore changing goals. The training process should be influenced by the dynamics of learning and business and attempt to keep pace with business changes.

In the strategy-planning subprocess of training, the intended learning strategies should be linked to the long-range goals of the organization. Training professionals need to answer the question, How will the training design result in knowledge and behavior that lead to performance improvement that achieves the goals of the organization?

In the subprocess for producing learning outcomes, training leaders need to ensure that what employees are learning is what they need to know to help the organization achieve its goals. If business needs change, employees lose sight of the purpose of the new knowledge and skills and training becomes a wasted effort. An example is the welding course that continues to be offered to factory line workers long after robots have taken over all the welding tasks on the production line.

The linkage after learning events have occurred is based on the extent to which trainees remain focused on important job performance objectives that can contribute to business needs and strategies. If the linkage breaks down after learning, then training-acquired skills, while they may endure, lose focus, causing employee performance to lose effectiveness. For example, in one sales training program, sales representatives learned powerful new techniques for establishing rapport with sales prospects and for closing sales. A part of the training strategy was that the sales reps would shift their attention to high-potential accounts in a "targeted marketing" approach that would allow the reps to spend more time with these clients and less time on less profitable accounts. A follow-up evaluation showed that the sales reps were indeed using their newly found "closing and rapport" skills, but they were also continuing to use the "shotgun" approach instead of the "targeted" approach. They were spending most of their time on the least productive accounts. The culprit was a combination of ineffective coaching from district managers and a perception among sales reps, which was confirmed by an inadvertent comment a senior manager made at a sales meeting, that promotions and rewards would continue to be based on high numbers reported in weekly call records. While the training goals had been clearly and strongly linked to primary business goals, this linkage had broken down and training was headed for failure.

To maintain linkage throughout the training process a number of actions must be taken. Training delivery modes and schedules must be integrated with strategic organizational structures. Learning interventions must include exercises that strengthen strategic linkage. Instructors must be sensitive to confusion among trainees about the relationship of training to strategic goals and find ways to clarify this linkage constantly. Supervisors of trainees must track progress toward linkage and act quickly to head off breakdowns. Follow-up evaluations of training's impact should highlight training's link to business success.

A number of techniques and tools have helped us enhance linkage throughout the subprocesses. Most of these have been derived from research on training effectiveness.

Formulating Training Goals

Fundamental questions need to be answered at the initiation of any training effort:

> Why is training needed?
> Where is training headed?
> What good will it do?
> How will we know whether it worked?

Getting stakeholders to devote the time necessary to answer these questions is not an easy task. Most of the time, we find training leaders overly anxious to jump into training events without knowing whether and how training will help their customers meet a need. While this usually eminates from a genuine desire to help and fulfill a request from someone else, the failure to link training to strategic goals leads to ineffective training and a waste of valuable company resources.

An example from our consulting experience illustrates the linking of training goals to strategic business goals. In this case, several days were devoted to analysis and clarification of the reasons why stakeholders wanted training and how that training could contribute to essential needs of the organization.

An international pharmaceutical manufacturing and marketing company, like its competitors, constantly seeks to reduce new drug development time. Its research and development investments are high, and there is no return on these investments until the new product is distributed in the marketplace. Accelerating the product development cycle enables the company to cut losses sooner if the drug is found to be unmarketable because it fails to meet the health risk standards of the Food and Drug Administration. The competition is fierce in this industry; the first company to reach the marketplace with a needed drug is usually the beneficiary of tremendous profits.

A small laboratory unit within the company had investigated ways in which it could contribute to faster development cycles. The primary work of this unit is conducting assays and other chemical tests for research scientists as part of quality control services. The quality lab identified two needs: (1) to reduce errors in in-process lab work and (2) to return test results to research scientists within shorter turnaround times.

As part of this performance improvement effort, the lab discovered that ineffective communications with its customers, the research scientists, was a key factor in both the errors and long turnaround times. Often, the lab workers first failed to understand the scientists' directions and then failed to interact with the scientists sufficiently while work was underway. The stakeholders decided that, in order to meet the needs of the lab's customers, the technicians needed improved communications skills. The belief was that training in these skills would lead to more efficient and accurate customer interactions, which should result in the unit achieving its ambitious objectives for accuracy and timeliness.

The pharmaceutical company's hierarchy of training, job performance, and unit and business goals that are linked to the organizational strategy are depicted below.

Strategic goal:	Improve competitiveness by getting the product to market more quickly
Business objective:	Reduce new product development time
Unit objectives:	Increase accuracy of lab work Decrease turnaround time on reports to scientists
Employee objectives:	Reduce errors in analysis Increase accuracy in understanding scientists' requirements
Learning objective:	Improve skills in communicating with

customers, including
listening, questioning, and
clarifying meaning

The linkage depicted here is between a specific learning objective for trainees and a high-level strategic goal. The intermediate objectives arrayed between the two indicate the intended logical and causal connections between elements. We call this analysis of linkage a linkage logic. From this analysis, one can develop an impact map (see Chapter Four) for the organization.

The clear depiction of linkage facilitates questioning and discussion about the validity of training goals. Those in the organization who are concerned with performance improvement can examine the rationale for the training and confirm or raise doubts about the logic. If the stakeholders in the pharmaceutical company had believed that the quality control functions of the lab did not contribute significantly to the drug development process, the training might have been based on faulty assumptions and therefore have resulted in a waste of effort. In fact, the company's analysis showed that a modest 10 percent reduction in lab processing time would result in a 0.5 percent reduction in overall development time, assuming that all other factors were held constant. This reduction translated into several hundred thousand dollars of savings, which easily justified the cost of training. The point is not whether the company's training plan was sound. Rather, the point is that the linkage analysis provided a focus for discussion of the logical underpinnings of the training goals.

Explicating linkage at the outset of any training development effort is critical regardless of whether training is intended to add value through immediate job performance, through the building of employee capacity to perform in the future, or through an enhanced workplace environment. The value of training is wasted when either the business goals that have been chosen are not the right goals for the organization or the training process will not help trainees achieve those goals. The articulation of the linkage enables training leaders and customers to discover whether either of these situations exists.

Over the long term, organizations can maintain linkage

through structured and extensive interaction with training customers. Some of the methods of interaction have been labeled front-end analysis, needs analysis, job analysis, and task analysis. These are step-by-step procedures for discovering the knowledge, skills, and attitudes that individuals need to help the organization achieve its goals. The analytical techniques have been well documented in the training literature (see Brinkerhoff, 1987, 1989; Goldstein, 1986; Harless, 1981; Mager, 1984b; Phillips, 1983; Robinson and Robinson, 1989; Rummler and Brache, 1991).

In the old learner-centered approach to training, the analysis methods are used to assess needs that emerge from the immediate performance and wishes of employees and often are influenced by current management fads. Tests, surveys, and structured observations of employees are used to assess deficits in knowledge and performance in relation to arbitrary standards set by vendors of equipment, developers of tests, and the latest thinking in industrial engineering. Employees are asked what they want to learn. Current management trends dictate what employees should be learning. These include quality circles, TQM, self-directed work teams, coaching and counseling, and diversity.

In the new system-focused approach, the needs of the organization drive the assessment. First, management must be clear about its goals and what it expects from employees to help reach those goals. Then gaps in performance or capacity to perform can be determined. This assessment, in relation to system needs, is what sets the parameters for training. Identifying these system needs requires the involvement of all the customers of training: users of the product or service, managers, and supervisors of trainees, as well as the trainees themselves.

One of the best ways to develop and sustain this involvement is by means of a training advisory committee. Comprised of key stakeholders, this committee represents the interests of the various groups affected by training and should meet regularly to review business and training needs. The advisory committee should advise training leaders on the collection and analysis of relevant data and provide guidance as to the allocation of the training investment. One or more members of the committee should serve as a human link between training and the strategic planning of senior management. The group can ensure that training decisions are responsive to and informed by business planning and that business planning is informed by perspectives on human performance. Serious business problems will arise if the organization embarks on a business plan that contains flawed assumptions about the levels of performance that can be achieved and sustained.

Linkage during the goal-setting subprocess is the cornerstone for linkage that occurs in the later phases of the training process. If goal linkage is weak, training efforts are likely to go in the wrong direction. When this happens, little can be done to get on the right path other than to start over again to build the linkage before training leaders begin to design training strategies. Linkage during the other subprocesses is important, but only to strengthen, nurture, and extend the primary linkage created during the goal-setting subprocess.

Planning Training Strategies

Linkage during the strategy planning subprocess refers not to the results of training but rather to the "how" of training. The emphasis is on the means by which training goals will be achieved. Training strategy defines and guides who will receive what kind of training, when it will be delivered, where it will be received, how it will operate, and who will manage the learning intervention.

Much of training strategy has been defined from a narrow instructional-design perspective driven mainly by a concern for creating the maximum amount of learning. While creating good learning conditions is certainly a vital concern of the training strategy, it is not the only, or even the most important, concern. A training design must do far more than produce learning. It must produce learning when it is most needed, for the most crucial employees, where the learning can be most effectively applied, and in a manner that supports achievement of the business goals. In short, the training design must be strategic.

Linking training strategies to business goals ensures that training will be carried out in a manner that is (1) integrated with the organization's work processes and culture and (2) likely to produce cost-effective, strategically valuable results. How important is this linkage? Consider the following example.

The CEO of a small manufacturing distribution business requested a review and an evaluation of his training operation. After interviews, observations, and analysis of training activities and their results, external consultants determined that the company had an outstanding training operation. Company employees, who were extremely productive and efficient, had helped the company achieve a record of customer service and loyalty that was superior to that of competitors. New employees were consistently provided with the skills they needed to contribute to company success. Older employees were given training that updated and enhanced their skills. Moreover, training costs were kept low. Nearly all the employees were satisfied with the training operation. In sum, there were no major flaws in the training operation given current business needs.

However, when the CEO received the report, it became apparent that the training operation needed a major overhaul. Existing training was producing all the right results for the company's current needs, but the CEO had plans for expanding the business. He wanted to increase the number of branch distribution centers from four to twenty-five over the following five years. In the company's present state, a training operation that took an average of six months to bring a new employee up to an excellent skill level was fully workable, turnover was low, and new business growth was at a pace that necessitated only minimal new hiring. However, under the new business plan for rapid expansion, the key factor that would determine growth rate was human resource development. The CEO could get the capital he needed to acquire buildings and materials for the branches relatively easily, but that was not sufficient. Staffing each new branch with capable people was critical to success. If training took six months for each branch, the new plan could not survive. The company would not be able to produce revenues quickly enough to underwrite capital expansion. The training cycle had to be reduced from six months to just four weeks.

Training in the pre-expansion environment was delivered mostly through a mentoring, on-the-job apprenticeship that unfolded over several months. The new training had to be far more compressed and intensified.

The new training strategy called for one of the company's branches to be a training facility where new branch employees could become rapidly immersed in business operations. The first few days of the tightly controlled and systematic training regimen put new trainees through self-paced knowledge aquisition modules, interspersed with observation of actual operations in the training branch. Trainees started with relatively simple tasks, such as filling out an order form or filling an order in the warehouse. Then, as their knowledge grew, they progressed to more complex tasks requiring more sophisticated knowledge and a broader understanding of business operations. Trainees moved through the training process as a team that would become the entire start-up staff for a new branch. By the end of four weeks, and sometimes sooner, the trainees were ready to move on to the newly opened branch, where they continued to receive instruction, coaching, feedback, and support. New branch operations were supported heavily by an elaborate system of job aids that provided detailed, step-by-step instruction in key tasks. As new staff gained experience, they weaned themselves away from the job aids. The training schedule was tied directly to the new business expansion schedule. In this way, the training strategy was able to support fully the business expansion and ensure successful growth.

This example shows why it is important for the training strategy to be fully aligned with the business strategy and operations. Alignment is also important in terms of the functioning of training services. For example, if a business strategy aims to build a high level of customer service, then training should likewise be built upon and reflect a strong customer service orientation. In this case, the customers of training are the trainees and their supervisors. The training design process should include opportunities for these customers to review the strategy and to judge the quality of training that is delivered.

Part of linking strategy planning to business goals is designing a way to make trainees aware of the linkage. They should know well in advance of a learning event the reasons for their participation in it, including how the training will benefit them and the company. In most situations, the linkage will have greatest impact if the trainees' immediate supervisors express it to them. Supervisors should do this in a way that creates a sense of enthusiasm, importance, and belief that the training can and will make a valuable difference. Trainers must also be fully informed about the linkage. They should be prepared to respond to questions and use examples that clarify and reinforce linkage of training goals and training strategy to the business goals of the organization.

To formulate a linked training strategy, professionals must answer these questions:

Who should receive the training interventions?
What kinds of training interventions fit the business strategy?
When should the training be delivered?
Who should be involved in delivering the training?

Obviously, these questions are not independent of each other. A well-planned training strategy must consider all these factors and their interrelationship at the same time.

At a general level, the "who" of training is decided when training goals are determined. For instance, if a training goal is to provide a sales force with knowledge about the company's new products, then it follows that the sales representatives should receive the training. However, further consideration might reveal that only certain sales representatives should be trained or that buyers of the product should be involved. The company's business plan helps determine the strategic issue of who should participate in training.

Sometimes the "who" of training is not quite as obvious. In these situations, more strategic thinking is called for. For instance, it may be best to begin training with participants who are most likely to succeed. Then training successes can be used to leverage more support and involvement from management. Or, it may be best to train intact cross-functional teams of employees because success depends on how well they work together and apply the knowledge and skills being taught.

In the old program-focused approach, the determinations of who receives training and when they receive it are driven by nonstrategic forces. What often happens is that employees enroll for particular programs out of personal interest or because their supervisors find out that seats are available. Then training is delivered to those who happen to be available regardless of the company's strategic concerns.

The trainee selection process should be strategic, not unmanaged or left to chance. Sometimes strategic concerns dictate that training should be provided to those who will most likely succeed, sometimes to those who are most needy, sometimes to those who are in areas where the risk to the company from participation is lowest, and sometimes where the risk of nontraining is greatest. A careful consideration of business needs should be made and then translated into a process for trainee selection.

Training practitioners have a vast array of learning technologies at their disposal. However, it is our experience that training developers rely heavily on a traditional classroom approach. This is due, in part, to a failure to link the method to strategic business goals. Emphasis is placed on the convenience and familiarity of the method rather than the needs of the organization. Depending on the business goals and feasibility, other methods such as mentoring, computer-based training, or benchmarking might be better methods of performance improvement than classroom instruction.

Good instructional design dictates that learning methods be matched with learning objectives. For example, if the learning objective is mastery of a specific skill, trainees may learn best by engaging in hands-on practice and performance trials. If the learning objective is application of specific personal interaction skills, a behavioral-modeling approach may be best. This matching of learning method to learning needs and objectives is a tactical decision. The extensive literature on instructional design can assist with this decision (Briggs, Gustafson, and Tillman, 1991; Gagne and Briggs, 1979; Mager, 1984a; Richey, 1986). However, the training leader should also address a number of strategic issues in selecting a method:

> To what extent can job aids or other expert-systems and information-access technologies be integrated into the training design?

Should training methods be mostly learner guided or trainer controlled?

Should trainees receive instruction in groups or individually?

To what extent can learning interventions be embedded into routine job operations, such as providing "help" screens in a computer-aided work activity?

When should learning checks and other feedback mechanisms be used?

How should training be scheduled?

Training interventions can take many different forms, depending on the answers to these questions. The following examples illustrate this point.

• Chemical process operators have jobs that call for intense periods of activity and periods with little to do. They may have to add ingredients to a large vat of brewing chemicals and alter the temperature of the vat. Then they may have to wait long periods of time for the next task. To take advantage of this downtime, safety training and new operations training were taken out of the classroom and put on computer diskettes. The workers now use portable computers during their downtime to upgrade their skills and refresh the knowledge that they need for the next week's work.

• Ford Motor Company has replaced considerable amounts of repair and maintenance training delivered via classroom sessions with training delivered via "smart kiosks." These are computers on stands in the repair bays of service garages. The computers are programmed with expert systems and other job aids to guide repair work, ensuring more timely and accurate service. This helps implement the company's strategy of cost reduction and enhanced customer service.

• New managers of branch offices of a temporary office personnel business receive job "survival" skills in a brief, classroom course prior to starting their new jobs. Then they participate in a series of visits to other branches, where they receive on-the-job instruction from "master" managers. This process increases the speed with which new managers are prepared to help their branches increase sales. At the same time, the process builds a network of contacts that helps all managers. This network aids the company's capacity to meet customer needs that cut across the territorial boundaries of each of the branch offices.

- The staff of a social service agency's administrative offices regularly observe other staff at work. While observing their peers, they fill out behavior checklists. Then each observer provides structured feedback to the trainee. This training strategy improves performance as staff learn from each other, reduces the time that is needed for classroom training, furthers the agency's goal of customer service excellence and accountability, and builds the capacity of staff to continuously improve their own performance, which is a state government mandate.

Following from the question about what kind of training is the question about when to deliver the training. Optimum scheduling of training entails consideration of the calendar, as in what months, weeks, or days the learning events should occur. But scheduling should also take into account the precise points in the business or operations cycle where training is needed. For example, in a sales training process, new information that had been provided to sales representatives in pre-assignment classroom instruction was redesigned to be delivered via laptop computer at the beginning of each quarterly market analysis period.

Scheduling of the sequence of training events is also important. Often, greater impact can be achieved simply by spreading out a series of learning events to allow for practice and feedback. For example, a program that had been delivered on three consecutive days was separated into smaller modules and delivered over a twelve-week period, increasing the impact of the training on performance in the workplace.

As much as possible, learning events should be delivered in the just-in-time manner discussed in Chapter Two. A major problem we have observed in many organizations is that training schedules are arranged to meet the administrative convenience and constraints of the training department rather than the critical business needs of the organization.

Part of the answer to the question of who should be involved in delivering training is the trainees themselves and those training leaders and facilitators required by the design of the training intervention. However, beyond these more obvious participants, other people should be involved for linkage reasons. A general rule of thumb is to seek broad involvement. As we have emphasized, when the various customers of training feel involved in its direction and success, they are more likely to view training as a resource that can help them achieve their goals.

Here are some examples of different types of customer involvement in the training process:

> The CEO of a company attends the first in a series of manager training sessions to answer questions and explain the business goals and strategies of the company.
>
> The supervisor of a trainee meets with the trainee and training leader before the learning event to agree to the specific job performance outcomes that are expected from training.
>
> External customers attend a meeting of service representatives to tell stories about how the company's service has affected them.
>
> A group of physicians meets with new pharmacuetical sales representatives to explain their needs, interests, values, and concerns.
>
> Experienced employees attend training sessions for new employees to describe how the training has helped them in their work.
>
> After a learning event, supervisors meet with trainees to review action plans for applying the training and to agree to a process for giving the trainees performance feedback.
>
> Senior managers meet to review and recommend changes to training goals and plans for each department.
>
> Representatives of the targeted trainees meet with the training developers to give their opinion about the design of the training process.

In each of these examples, involvement of the various customers has a specific strategic purpose intended to create or strengthen linkage.

Producing Learning Outcomes

Training methods and activities should reinforce the linkage of training with business goals and strategy. To a large extent, the methods and activities for a particular performance improvement system are defined during the planning of training strategies. During the third subprocess, these plans are carried out and monitored to ensure that they are producing the desired outcome, that is, that linkage to strategic goals is maintained and reinforced.

Practices that we have found to be useful in reinforcing linkage throughout the implementation of training include the following:

- Publishing training documents, such as announcements and schedules, that clearly indicate and emphasize how training is linked to business goals and strategic initiatives
- Ensuring communication between trainees and their supervisors, particularly during learning events, that reinforces learning and plans for application to the job
- Establishing a process of accountability for improved performance that includes progress toward achieving strategic goals
- Providing continuous feedback on all aspects of the training process
- Arranging publicity for successful learning methods and their contribution to achieving business goals
- Discussing linkage in every learning event

Supporting Performance Improvement

This subprocess is critical to longterm linkage. Training, if done effectively, will have immediate effects on performance. However, short-term results are no guarantee that trainees will continue to apply new knowledge and behaviors. Learning must be reinforced periodically. This is less of a concern for skills such as interpersonal communication that are usually used every day, and much more of a concern for skills such as safety, project management, and the use of various software programs that might not be used for weeks or months.

One mechanism for reinforcement during this subprocess is supervisor involvement. As with the other phases of the training process, supervisors can strengthen the link between training and achieving business goals by discussing this linkage with trainees and holding them accountable for learning that will benefit the organization. Another mechanism for reinforcement is refresher learning events. These are repeated training activities to remind trainees of the knowledge and skills they were taught earlier. Part of these events should be to remind trainees of how the training is related to business success. Yet another reinforcement mechanism is continuous measurement of the impact of training. The process of measurement will bring attention to training and its relationship to business success, and the feedback from this measurement can lead to improving the linkage. Such measurement also allows for a reassessment of training needs. Trainees' needs may have changed, business needs may have changed, or perhaps the needs were not accurately assessed in the first place.

Summary

The first principle of the new approach to performance improvement is to link training to the business goals and strategies of the organization. This linkage ensures that training will add value to the products and services of the business. To be effective the linkage must be developed and maintained throughout the training process. The HET approach to training described in Chapter One provides a useful framework for explaining and giving examples of linkage throughout training. In the first subprocess, formulating training goals, the relationship of a desired training outcome to a strategic business goal must be demonstrated. The key to this subprocess is getting stakeholders involved in deciding what knowledge, skills, attitudes, and beliefs are needed by employees to help the company be successful. In the second subprocess, planning training strategies, learning methods are selected that will result in the outcomes necessary for achieving the strategic objectives. The third subprocess, producing learning outcomes, involves implementing training methods and activities. Linkage must be maintained throughout this subprocess or participants will lose focus on the purpose of learning. The fourth subprocess, supporting performance improvement, depends on continual reinforcement of learning and the link between learning and strategic objectives. Supervisor involvement, refresher learning events, and measurement are some of the tools for providing this reinforcement.

The next chapter discusses the second principle of the new approach to training: maintaining a strong customer service focus.

7

Maintaining Customer Focus

Customer needs and expectations are the key to quality. When a product or service meets or exceeds these needs and expectations, it has quality. When a product or service falls short of customer needs and expectations, by definition, quality standards are not met. This inextricable knitting together of customers and quality drives the need for training to build and maintain a strong customer focus.

This chapter explains the mandate for a customer focus and offers guidelines and procedures for ensuring that training continuously meets customer needs and exceeds customer expectations. The first part of the chapter reviews the role of customers in quality management and explains why a customer service perspective is critical for highly effective training. The second part describes a number of strategies that training leaders can employ to link training to customer needs and ensure the most effective training services.

Quality and Customer Service

Although the concepts of quality and customer service are inextricably linked, we have separated them for the sake of clarity in this discussion. All approaches to TQM stress the critical role of the customer in first defining what we mean by quality and then being instrumental in maintaining quality (Bowles and Hammond, 1991). A common definition of quality in a product or service is "fit for use by the customer." Such a product or service has been designed to meet the usage demands of the customer. In terms of training, internal and external customers should be able to apply what they have learned in training to improving their performance. For example, if a manager in a computer repair business needs employees to troubleshoot common problems of a Compustar 500, the quality of the training should be judged by how well the employees can locate any problems and make repairs in that computer. If some trainees do not acquire these skills, the customer's needs have not been met and quality standards have not been achieved.

Although this definition of quality puts the focus where it rightfully belongs, squarely on customer needs and expectations, it does not convey the difficulty often encountered in determining customer needs. Companies that manufacture consumer products have learned that they must take elaborate measures to ensure that their design teams hear "the voice of the customer." For example, American automobile manufacturers suffered in the past because their designers were out of touch with the customer. They built cars that met key engineering specifications but missed the mark on what customers wanted. The production and demise of the Ford Edsel is a classic example of this phenomenon.

In the past ten years, the auto companies have made dramatic changes toward putting quality and customer needs first. The Cadillac Division of General Motors (a recent Baldrige Award winner) is a good example of this. Cadillac engineers placed their cars in shopping malls and had teams of design engineers observe the results. While potential customers crawled around and into the cars, the engineers asked them what they liked and disliked about the cars. In short, the engineers learned what customers wanted and expected in a high-quality car.

The difficulty of determining customer needs and expectations is evident in all training because there are so many customers of training and their needs are not always the same. Sometimes they may even be in conflict. New sales trainees, for instance, may want product orientation and training in selling skills to last until they are confident that they will be successful in the field. District managers, also customers of training, want skilled sales representatives, but they want people covering the sales territories even more.

Training leaders must be adept at identifying the multiple customers of training and then understanding their several needs. When conflicts arise, which is inevitable, the training leaders must try to understand these differences and then move to resolve the conflict. For example, they might facilitate a goal-setting session that includes new sales reps and their district managers. Although training may not meet everyone's needs and trade-offs must be made, quality is threatened when competing interests interfere with goal clarity.

Another problem with identifying customer needs is that training customers may not know or be able to articulate their needs. They may be able to express superficial wishes and wants but not be aware of what they need to learn to be more effective in their jobs. This requires a level of insight and self-assessment that not everyone has.

When employees do become clear about their needs, those needs might not be what another customer, such as their supervisor, wants. An example of this is a situation in which the manager of the telemarketing department of one company requested conflict management training for supervisors. This manager had observed a number of serious arguments and nonproductive gripe sessions because the workers disagreed with the work procedures. They were being required as a group to achieve minimum call-answering goals and call-per-hour completion rates. An analysis of call-waiting and call-duration data showed that problems were only occurring early in the morning on certain weekdays. However, the arguing and griping went on all week. Further analysis revealed that staffing patterns, not supervisors' lack of conflict management skills, were causing the failure to meet goals. Operator performance standards were based on average calls per week, which masked peak calling periods caused by market conditions. The solution was to hire part-time help two mornings per week. As a result, performance standards were met and arguments and griping ended. Gone was the "need" for training.

In this case, discovering that the need was a structural one, not a performance need, was relatively simple. However, many customer needs are less apparent, requiring analysis beyond the immediate workplace. Another example, taken from the home health care telemarketing group described earlier, illustrates this point. In this instance, customer needs related to improving the rate of calls converted into actual sales. The targeted rate had been determined by a business analysis and goals for profits and for return on assets. Moreover, an industry benchmark study of call conversion ratios was also conducted. All managers in the organization agreed with the analysis and were committed to the performance standards. When the performance data showed slippage in the call conversion rates, training in call efficiency and sales skills seemed needed. This training was endorsed by management.

Then a senior marketing manager, newly hired from outside the company, reviewed the training plan. She reported that the plan conflicted with what she was beginning to see as a shift in market forces. A new high-tech industrial park had recently opened in the company's telemarketing area, bringing with it a more senior workforce of a higher socioeconomic status than that of the rest of the marketing area. This represented a growing new market: families caring for their elderly parents at home. This new market required considerable coaching and rapport building on the part of the telephone sales staff. The potential customers felt guilty about hiring out services that they felt they should be providing themselves. To become successful in this new market segment, the company needed to adopt new sales standards and procedures.

Because training in call efficiency and sales skills was needed for short-term profitability, it was still conducted, but it was modified to prepare phone operators for the new market segment. Sales people were introduced to new call-answering protocols and standards that will be more appropriate in the near future.

In this example, the true needs of the training customer were deeply embedded in the business context. Even a business and training needs analysis did not uncover the knowledge and skills that would result in performance improvement. Not until an expanded market analysis was conducted did the organization become clear about the best direction for training.

Training leaders are often caught in a bind when it comes to meeting customer needs. On one hand, if a training leader responds to a customer's initially articulated need, quality may be threatened. The customer may not be immediately aware of his or her true need and any response may therefore be a wasted effort. On the other hand, if training leaders ignore the expressed need and dig relentlessly deeper for the "true" need, the cooperation of the sometimes desperate customer may be lost. The way out of this apparent dilemma is to have a comprehensive understanding of customer needs and a systematic approach to needs analysis, review, negotiation, and agreement. HET depends on the design and delivery of training that meets customer needs—and thereby makes quality possible.

Training as a Customer Service

The concepts and practices of customer service are valuable leverage points for producing highly effective training. The common business wisdom is that the battleground for profits has shifted from manufacturing and product quality to customer service (Albrecht and Zemke, 1985; Davidow, 1989). As global competition and wide access to information have diminished the quality differences in basic products, customers are increasingly making decisions on the basis of how they are treated.

The field of human resource development can benefit greatly from this service viewpoint and its supporting technologies. Training is not a product; it is a service. We say this despite the many tangible elements of a training intervention, such as three-ring binders for trainees, instructional guides for trainers, self-assessment instruments, audiotapes, videotapes, videodiscs, computer software, and more. Training customers do not want to purchase these training resources, however; they want to purchase the results of training. If they could buy the results, they would readily forego the training.

The customer service concept posits that all service companies add value to their "core service" by all the secondary services that they provide. For example, a car detailer's core service is cleaning cars, and a hotel's core service is providing a room to sleep in overnight. But if all these businesses did was perform their core services, they would not meet customer expectations and could not be competitive. The car detailer comes to the customer's home or office, asks for special cleaning requests from the customer, fills the car with gas and windshield wiper fluid, and makes suggestions for better car care. The hotel provides cable TV, turns down the covers on the bed, leaves a chocolate mint on the pillow, and delivers a newspaper and coffee to the room in the morning. All these secondary services enrich the perceived value of the service to the customer. Excellence in customer service is achieved when providers understand their customers' contexts, pressures, hopes, foibles, and concerns and then help their customers receive increasingly more value from the core service.

In performance improvement systems, the core service is *learning*. Learning is the primary result of training interventions, be they seminars, self-instructional packages, workshops, on-the-job training sessions, or mentoring. However, learning alone adds little value, as discussed elsewhere in this book. Improved job performance comes about when learning interventions, the core service of training, are integrated within a larger set of value-adding services. For example, sales representatives in the pharmaceutical company described earlier must be able to provide technical assistance to physicians who may prescribe the company's products. In this organization, product training for sales representatives is critical to all types of customers, including the end users of the product. Thus training professionals developed product information modules that the sales reps could readily access on their laptop computers. This innovation is an example of a peripheral customer service that adds considerable value to the trainers' core service, product learning. Sales reps can acquire product knowledge when and where they need it and in the amount that they need. This training service reduces costs to the sales department by reducing in-house training time. The service also increases the accuracy and timeliness of product information as module updates are provided regularly in the form of new diskettes. Moreover, the service provides the patient, the ultimate customer, with more accurate and efficacious prescriptions.

The sales training intervention has augmented the customer's ability to get maximum value from the core product. This is an example of customer service from training leaders that meets a variety of customers' needs. Value was added to the core service for the trainee, and this value was extended to meet the needs of physicians and patients.

Secondary services need not be elaborate to have considerable impact on customers. One training department leader makes it a habit to telephone a few trainees and their supervisors after each learning intervention. She simply asks them whether the training experience has helped them and whether her department can do anything else to help them be successful in their work. In another case, employees who receive project management training can have their project management plans reviewed by graduate students in a project management class at a local university. Within two weeks, the students write constructive critiques of the plans and then send them to the trainees. The trainees are delighted with this extra service, and the university students benefit from the "real world" consultation experience.

Customer service, in its core and secondary forms, is a powerful tool for achieving the goals of HET. Applying a systems approach to measuring and understanding customer needs and then using value-adding activities before, during, and after the learning events contribute great leverage to efforts to produce truly valuable and sustaining results from training.

Customer Service Strategies

In this section we discuss a number of customer service strategies that training leaders can readily implement. These strategies will not only immediately add value but also create a customer service culture within the performance improvement system. This culture will continue to add increased value over time.

Identify Training Customers, Ask Them the Right Questions, and Get to Know Their Needs and Expectations

Training's many customers have different needs and expectations. If training quality depends on giving customers what they need, then training leaders must first know who these customers are. Descriptions of the various categories of training customers are presented in Chapter Five. The list includes managers and supervisors of trainees, trainees, senior management, organizational support staff, and external customers (suppliers, end users of the company's product or service, and others affected by the training).

Training leaders should not assume that they know their customers. The task of identifying customers and their different needs is a valuable process for the training organization to go through. The process forces the training organization to answer questions such as, What business are we in? Who do we want to be serving? What are we currently doing for those customers? The value-adding component of customer identification lies largely in the process of interacting with customers, getting to know them, expressing concern and interest, asking questions, and listening to their answers.

Segment Training Markets and Tailor Services to Them

Product and service industries have learned that a key to competitive advantage lies in identifying and defining the particular needs of each market segment. This is dramatically different from the traditional "shotgun" approach, where a product or service is distributed as widely as possible to get enough "hits" to make it profitable. For example, a society matron's housecleaning needs and expectations are different from those of a single parent working two jobs. A competitive housecleaning franchise will segment its market to identify such different customer groups. Then the business will target its core services and service peripherals at these different market segments.

Market segmentation fits training just as well as any other service. We have already pointed out the pitfalls and shortcomings of a one-size-fits-all approach to training. This approach fails to add optimum value precisely because it does not segment the training market.

For example, a large financial institution has hundreds of computer stations and users. An initial analysis of the needs of these users showed a great deal of commonality among software applications. Nearly two-thirds of the users were using the same widely known spreadsheet program. In response to the wide use of that program, the training department frequently offered workshops on the software. The demand for the workshops was great, the workshops were full and conducted by skilled trainers, and the waiting lists for the sessions kept growing. This was stressful for the training staff and frustrating for the waiting trainees and their supervisors.

Evaluation of the workshops showed that trainees learned the content. However, the evaluation also showed the following:

Trainees required considerable assistance after the learning event.

Performance on the job was not meeting supervisors' expectations.

Trainees knew more than they needed to know about the software in general but did not know how to apply it to their specific tasks.

There was general and widespread displeasure with the training department because employees had a vague perception that the department was providing inferior service.

The problem was a one-size-fits-all mentality that drove the training design and delivery. In an effort to be fair, the training department allocated a few seats to each department in the company. In an effort to be comprehensive and provide something for everyone, the workshops were packed with information about all aspects of the software and its operation. In an effort to give everyone some practice in the session, the training staff had created brief, generic application exercises to which all trainees would identify. For instance, one exercise was preparing a budget for an office picnic. The workshops did not include any job-specific practice applications that showed trainees how to use the software in their home departments. The training design and delivery precluded the knowledge and skills that employees needed most.

The solution lay in segmenting markets and then targeting training to each segment. This resulted in the development of nine different workshops, each specific to a common job function, such as Using Spreadsheet Applications in Retail Sales and Spreadsheet Applications for Investment Planning. The market segments were identified by careful analysis of department operations and needs, and trainees were encouraged to bring job-specific problems to the workshops.

The result was training events that were shorter, allowing more frequent demand-driven sessions. Trainees learned only what they needed to do to use the software for important tasks. The training department operated a troubleshooting hot line that provided follow-up consultation to support on-the-job transfer of learning. Overall training costs were reduced, and results improved dramatically as trainees made immediate applications back in their offices. Finally, the attitudes of trainers and their customers also improved.

Incorporate Measurement as the First and Last Steps in a Customer Service Effort

Customer service begins with being knowledgeable about the different customers. This knowledge comes from measurement of customer attitudes and opinions, the job context, needs, and performance.

Measurement data affected the decisions that were made in the financial services company described above. Following are some of the measures that were used:

> Simple counts of the types of spreadsheet applications that were made during the previous year
>
> Postworkshop surveys of trainees regarding difficulty they were having using the spreadsheet application in their jobs
>
> Monthly hot-line data summaries that tracked the number and nature of calls and problems encountered by users
>
> Proportion of trainees who mastered each of the training objectives and their application
>
> Number of errors discovered in spreadsheet applications in each business department

The use and analysis of measurement data ensure that training providers interact with their customers in a detailed and focused manner. This interaction is intended to build the knowledge base for understanding the problems and issues customers face. However, measurement serves other equally important functions. It helps service providers and customers come to agreement on the things that "count," as well as the things that can be counted. In this way, measurement helps create a focus on goals and builds commitment to achieve those goals. Initial measurement of customer needs helps identify market segments and provides a reference point for gauging the success and impact of training services. Measurement of the delivery and outcomes of learning activities helps monitor the effectiveness of new learning events and makes incremental improvements in the entire training process. Finally, measurement data help training leaders and their customers see the final results and plan for the future. Measurement is discussed in more detail in Chapter Nine, which is dedicated to the fourth principle of HET.

Build Training Infrastructure for Maintaining Customer Communications and Involvement

As discussed earlier, training has become increasingly distanced from training customers in today's organization. The old paradigm view of training, prevalent among training professionals as well as management, holds that the mission of training is to provide training programs and products. Trainers will know whether they are successful by attendance in the programs. This paradigm suggests minimal customer service infrastructure.

When a shift is made to the emerging paradigm, the training mission becomes one of solving employees' performance and business problems. This mission necessitates new and different training infrastructures. Long-term organizational structures that connect training leaders and performance improvement systems to customers should be established. These may take the form of communication channels, committee memberships, team involvement, and leadership positions. Initial efforts to engage in highly effective training will require inventive means to establish contact with key customer groups. Actions outside routine communication and authority channels will be necessary.

Some infrastructure elements pertain broadly to all the training efforts of an organization. Here are some examples of these general elements:

- A training leader permanently placed on the organization's long-range strategic planning committee

- A business policy that mandates collaboration between senior management and training leaders
- A training approval process that requires reviews by standing committees and individuals representing management
- A permanent unit in the training organization that is accountable for customer satisfaction
- A senior management group to whom the training organization is accountable
- A tracking system for performance improvement costs that is reviewed by customer groups
- A customer feedback system that pinpoints training-related issues and reports them to training leaders

Some infrastructure elements are specific to training efforts for particular market segments. Examples of these specific elements include the following:

- A hot-line service for training issues and concerns of a particular employee group
- Managers who act as trainers or small group leaders in a learning event because of their expertise
- A cross-functional group of line employees who advise training leaders on training needs

Because even so-called "permanent" structural innovations tend to deteriorate over time, they need regular evaluation, nurturing, and rejuvenation. Participants need to be reminded of the purpose and importance of these organizational activities.

Create and Implement a Comprehensive Customer Service Strategy for Training

A customer service strategy for training should permeate and shape all aspects of the training process. The strategy should mandate that customer needs and expectations be assessed through measurement and extensive interactions with customers. The strategy should not be the result of training staff members brainstorming ideas and making guesses about needs; nor should the strategy be dictated by training vendors of packaged programs.

A customer service strategy should provide for customer review of all aspects of the training process. Representatives of customer groups should react to the needs analysis, goals, evaluation plan, strategies for learning, implementation plan, and what will be done to add value to the training process over time.

A service strategy for training should shape policies within the training department. In one company, the policy is that trainers have experience in the business area in which they provide services. When these employees are selected, they are told that they must be involved in at least two business projects each year with their customers and that their customers will review and provide input for the trainers' performance appraisals.

In another company, the customer service strategy has shaped the scheduling and assignment of training staff. They are required to spend a documented 25 percent of their time in direct customer interactions. In these interactions, trainers and unit managers discuss needs and the training activities.

In yet another company, a training process that includes learning events on customer service and listening skills has been developed for the training staff. This company does not assume that trainers have good customer service abilities. Moreover, the training staff are given "sabbaticals" in line departments to help them better understand the business and needs of their customers.

A customer service strategy may also influence the organization of training staff. In one company, the human resource development department had been organized for many years by specialty areas. The department had a management development group, a recruiting and hiring group, a technical skills group, and other specialists. The new customer service strategy called for a reorganization. Instead of specialty areas, the staff were reassigned to teams that had responsibility for meeting the needs of specific business operations. Training specialists are required to interact with other employees to design business solutions to performance problems and needs. Project success is determined by comparing results of training events to the customer's needs and expectations. Performance appraisals of training staff start with the customer and then are reviewed by human resource managers, with the final sign-off by customers.

A comprehensive service strategy must also drive activities that influence customer expectations for training. Line employees and management often have unrealistic expectations for what learning events, by themselves, can accomplish. Everyone in the organization needs help in keeping his or her desire for training within realistic boundaries. Through close involvement with needs analysis and evaluation, in particular, training leaders can help training customers see the limitations and possibilities of training. They can help customers see that learning events are only part of the larger performance improvement picture. (See Chapter Eight for elaboration on this point.) Only when training's customers understand the nature of training in an organizational context and their key role in ensuring lasting results, can truly effective customer service be achieved.

Engineer Quality Service into Training by Design

Quality service cannot be achieved by follow-up activities, such as troubleshooting, retraining, or other "inspection and repair" procedures. Again, we can borrow from the quality product concepts now being applied in automobile manufacturing. All successful automakers today have learned that a service strategy must permeate all operations of their business, whether that is engineering a part for the drivetrain or marketing a new car-leasing program. Before the days of intense competition with Japanese automakers, U.S. companies defined customer service as an after-purchase activity. For example, they would attempt to satisfy consumers with expensive warranties and friendly service departments in dealerships. Such practices drove up the cost of quality and left a disappointed consumer market vulnerable to competitors who could provide higher quality in the sales and product experience. The current view is that quality service must be designed into engineering, manufacturing, marketing, sales, and all other operations. This customer service strategy has profoundly altered the design process, maximizing interactions between designers, engineers, suppliers, and management. The old approach of serial design, where a different group designs each part of the car and then all the designs are turned over to manufacturing to produce, is changing. It is being replaced by cross-functional teams that involve people from all aspects of the business at the earliest point possible, even at the point where the car is just a concept. All team members have access to consumer input and use this information to create a design and a total car that will be competitive in its market.

The major implication for the training process is that to be effective, strategic planners cannot hand over their work to human resource development professionals, who then hand off their work to instructional developers, who then give their course materials to training leaders, who then deliver a course to trainees. In many organizations, the process is like the old parlor game in which a phrase is whispered from ear to ear sequentially along a line of people. The group rocks with hilarity when the last person in line says out loud something totally different from what the first person had whispered. In the human performance business this is not funny. The results of this kind of serial process are inevitable: an inferior training process and products, disappointed customers, and high costs.

Nevertheless, people continue to work in a serial process. Senior managers spend secluded months in strategic planning and major organizational restructuring. Human resource directors are brought in after the planning has concluded and told the implications for their department. This is communicated to the training staff, who have been hearing frightening rumors for months. They are directed to produce the appropriate training programs. Whoever's turn it is to attend a national human resource development convention is sent with instructions to collect any material related to the new program topics being considered. Then that person cruises the convention's exhibit hall seeking an affordable and attractive package from the hordes of training vendors. She or he makes a selection and, once back in the office, submits the selection for approval and a purchase order. Finally, with the program in hand, the training leaders schedule sessions for their customers.

Although this scenario is a mild exaggeration, it is very similar to the story we hear from many organizations. This process is costly and not likely to meet customers' needs. A concurrent process would be far less costly and have a much higher return on invest-ment. A concurrent process means engaging customers at the begin-ning, involving HRD professionals in the business planning of the organization, and keeping customers involved in every part of the training process.

Summary

A strong customer focus in training is part of a comprehensive approach to producing highly effective training. A customer focus means that the needs and expectations of all customers are met. It also means that customers become involved in the entire training process, from the initial concept to the transfer and maintenance of learning in the workplace. The revolution in service quality throughout business and industry provides training leaders with a powerful set of rules and procedures to design and manage the training process. Customer service will add value to training's core product: learning that works to improve performance. At the center of effective customer service is a comprehensive customer service strategy that shapes the training organization and all aspects of training operations.

In the next chapter we explore how systems thinking keeps the entire organization focused on the learning needs of training customers.

8

Using Systems Thinking
to Integrate
Work and Learning

One of the primary reasons why the training myths discussed in Chapter Three have become accepted is that training in organizations has been compartmentalized. Training has been shaped by an old paradigm that separates the training function operationally from the central business activities, as if human performance is an independent aspect of organization life.

In this chapter we describe the third principle of HET: manage training with a systems view of learning in the organization. This principle has its foundation in systems thinking. The chapter starts with a brief analysis of the old way of thinking about training, then explores some of the forces and practices that keep training separated from the mainstream of organizational life, and next explains systems thinking and why this way of thinking about organizations is essential to achieving highly effective training. Finally, the chapter presents practical process management as a practical solution to some of the problems that the absence of a systems approach has created.

The Separation of Work and Learning

The industrial revolution was made possible by the specialization of work and workers. As production became more complicated and organizations became more complex, tasks were assigned to departments and to specialists within those departments. This pattern was probably necessary given the times and certainly resulted in tremendous productivity gains and financial success for many large companies. Henry Ford's assembly line is an example of this specialization. The assembly process was separated into discrete activities, and a worker's job was to perform one specific task on each automobile. This enabled mass production and resulted in an affordable automobile for the masses.

As industries grew, they became more and more compartmentalized. A typical medium- to large-size manufacturing business today is separated into administration, operations (including purchasing and manufacturing), marketing and sales, communications and public relations, research and development, finance, and human resources. Then, depending on the size of the company, these departments are further separated into many smaller functional units. For example, the human resource area is often subdivided into personnel, employee relations, staff benefits, and training. Sometimes these units grow up totally independently of each other. Special initiatives will cause the formation of additional departments, albeit temporary, such as quality, empowerment, diversity, fitness, and safety.

The result of this specializing of work and compartmentalizing of business functions has been the separating of work from the learning process. The conventional wisdom of the industrial and postindustrial ages has been that people make things "at work" and learn things "in school"; a person's identity comes from either a work role (inside or outside the home) or a school role; students are young and workers are older; people complete their education, begin a career, retire, and only then begin studying the topics that are interesting and enjoyable to them. Even though, in reality, this scenario has many exceptions, it is a way of thinking about work and learning that has guided the organization of our schools and workplaces and continues to shape national policy.

Business and industry have structured worker education according to the traditional school model. However, schools, both public and private, have been organized almost exclusively for a customer who is five to eighteen years of age and attends classes of twenty to thirty-five children in grades kindergarten through twelve. Although demographics are changing, the norm is still undergraduate education for eighteen- to twenty-two-year-olds and graduate courses for twenty-two- to thirty-year-olds. Instruction is delivered within disciplines, during quarters or semesters, for two, three, or four hours of credit. Even the nontraditional and flexible programs of community-based adult education and many community colleges deliver instruction within traditional disciplines and time slots. Their method of delivery, such as classroom lecture, recitation, and read-test-read-test, has not changed substantially in the last 100 years.

This approach to education, separate from work and delivered in classrooms within a predetermined length of time, has influenced the training function throughout the public and private sectors. We realize that there are many exceptions, some cited in this book, but this is still by far the predominant approach to training today. The fact that this approach is not effective for most training has not done much to challenge the conventional wisdom.

A separate training function made much more sense in an essentially industrial and manufacturing economy. In that environment, many of the tasks required of workers could be learned in relatively brief training sessions and through a little on-the-job practice and would then be performed over and over for years. People could learn any job in six months or less because of training. This gave immigrants and many others access to jobs in industry. Training was used to provide workers with the minimum technical skills to perform a specific task, not to develop their abilities to advance themselves within their industries.

Now that we are entering the "knowledge age" (Drucker, 1992) and we are becoming "knowledge workers" (Peters, 1992), we are shifting from a world of work based on what a person can do to what a person knows and how that person can use information. Carnevale (1990), in a study he did for the American Society for Training and Development and the U.S. Department of Labor, concluded that the new economy needs workers with a much broader and deeper range of knowledge than is currently required. The organizations that will be competitive in the new economy will be those with workers who can use their brainpower to learn how to apply new technologies and solve complex problems.

In this knowledge era, separating work from learning is dysfunctional. There are fewer and fewer jobs wherein workers can be trained in a task that they will perform for the next several years. Most jobs today change within a matter of months, not years. Jobs are changed by new technology, by competition, and by new ways of managing organizations. The worker who was hired for a strong back and a positive attitude belongs to a dying breed. The new worker must be able to manage information, communicate effectively, think creatively, and solve problems. This causes greater dependence on the educational process, both inside and outside the workplace. However, this increasing need for learning cannot be effectively addressed as long as work and learning are separated.

The departmental structure of the training function has the effect of separating learning from work. The creation of training departments was probably inevitable. As the workplace evolved into a complex, dynamic, and knowledge-driven environment, businesses needed people to manage the many aspects of human resource development. Companies recognized the need for training and, in typical fashion, solved this problem by creating new departments. In their haste to deal with the growing need, however, they took the responsibility for training and development away from supervisors and managers and relieved other departments of having to deal with that aspect of the business.

Now more than ever training is being separated physically and psychologically from other business functions. Many major corporations, such as Aetna, the U.S. Postal Service, Xerox, Motorola, and Arthur Anderson, have built large, state-of-the-art, autonomous training facilities. Many other organizations have centralized training into its own unit, sometimes in the corner or wing of a production building but more often in the lush confines of the corporate administrative headquarters.

Given the enormous investment that companies have made in a separated training function, it is no wonder that training leaders rarely seem to apply systems thinking to their work. Yet learning and knowledge are not commodities that can be produced in one place and then consumed in another. Learning is not a resource to be tapped like maple syrup and then carried to the workplace to be served whenever the job could use a little sweetening. Learning is a process, inextricably woven into living and working.

The task before training leaders who want to implement highly effective training is to overcome the barriers that keep learning separated from the mainstream of the organization's work. These barriers are imposing, for they are built on the long-standing traditional views of school-based education and they are rooted in the traditional organizational structures of large businesses. The tools and concepts of systems thinking are sufficiently powerful to help training leaders overcome these barriers. Free of them, training leaders can promote a highly effective approach to training, where learning becomes integrated into the everyday process of work.

Systems Thinking

The systems approach is not new. It emerged from the problem-solving efforts of scientists and engineers during World War II (Churchman, 1968). On the one hand, systems thinking is a simple logic that anyone can use to manage the complexities of life. On the other hand, it is "rocket science"; NASA could not put astronauts in space without systems thinking.

A system is a network of functional elements that operate interdependently to produce a result. This definition applies as much to a hand-held calculator as it does to national health care. An example close to home is a gas heating system. The output, or goal, of this heating system is to maintain a comfortable temperature and level of humidity. The major elements of the system are a source of fuel (such as a gas line), a furnace, air ducts or water pipes, a blower or pump, and a thermostat. Each part has a particular job to do: the thermostat measures the temperature in the house and sends a message to the furnace to turn on or off, a flame element in the furnace burns the fuel, the furnace captures the heat from the burning fuel, the blower (if air system) or the pump (if water system) forces the heat out of the furnace, and the ducts or pipes transfer the heat throughout the house.

In this system, all parts must operate effectively in order for the goal to be achieved. If the gas line is clogged, the furnace will have nothing to burn even though the thermostat is asking for more heat. If the thermostat is broken and cannot accurately measure the temperature, it will cause too little or too much heat to be sent out.

By adding a human element to our example, the home heating system becomes much more similar to an organizational training scenario. For example, someone in the house intervenes in the system by selecting a new temperature on the thermostat. Now the system's goal is defined by this person, and the system operates to achieve this goal: to warm or cool the house to the selected temperature. Each of the elements of the heating system responds to the new goal because of the interdependence of all the elements.

Our simple heating system quickly becomes more complex when we introduce the human element. The goals keep shifting as the needs of people in that environment change. If, like us, you have had out-of-town visitors as houseguests, you understand how the heating system must respond to a variety of demands. Using programmable thermostats, we can set the temperature lower during the day, higher in the evenings, and then lower again at night. This serves us well, given our lifestyles, but it does not meet the needs of guests, especially those who are not used to our cold Michigan winters. So we must make changes to accommodate our guests. We could continue to control the system by using feedback (such as complaints) from our houseguests and adjust the thermostat accordingly. This is a very inefficient way to change the system, however. A more efficient means would be to show (train) our visitors how to use the thermostat. This training adds a new element to our system. If we have frequent visitors, a simple job aid could be used to instruct visitors in how to adjust the system, in which case we would need only point out the thermostat's location.

Additional system elements that make the system more complex than it first appears could come into play. What if there is a severe fuel shortage? If our guests turn the thermostat up, we could experience greatly increased fuel bills and risk running out of fuel. In this case, we would try to find alternative solutions to the problem of making our guests comfortable, such as asking them to wear extra clothing or to stay at a local hotel.

The point of this example is that system goals require occasional review as internal and external conditions change. How a problem is solved depends on how we define the goal of the system. If the goal in our homes is to keep the temperature constant, that requires one kind of solution. If the goal is to make our guests comfortable, that requires another kind of solution. And if the goal is to keep the temperature as low as possible without posing a risk to the house, our guests, or ourselves, then that requires still another solution.

Systems are not only affected by their own internal changing needs and goals, but they are also affected by external factors. All systems are influenced by the systems around them. Our home heating system is affected by worldwide fuel production and distribution, national environmental policy, weather, personal economics, and many other factors.

Take a brief flight of imagination with us. Suppose that the elements of our home heating example have some personality. On the surface the system appears to be mechanical and electrical and can be explained by physics, but underneath, each element has a mind of its own. Now it is more like a human organization. Imagine all the things that can pose problems for our heating system:

> The burner element is tired from constantly cycling on and off during an especially cold night and does not want to hold its flame the next day.
> The thermostat is confused about the complicated instructions it has been getting and delivers the lowest heat level when we want it the warmest.
> The fuel tank, having received recognition for being full, decides to stay full as long as possible and refuses to release the amount of fuel being requested by the thermostat.
> The blower talks the furnace into staying on longer, which gives the blower more time to rest.
> The heat ducts, having received little attention, begin to rattle and vibrate, making loud noises throughout the house.

Do you recognize these "people" in your system? The mechanical and electrical heating system can be diagrammed on paper and its performance predicted with great accuracy. The human element makes the system much more complicated and much less predictable.

Applying Systems Thinking to Training

Two major subsystems affect training success: (1) components internal to the training process, such as needs, objectives, learning modules, instruction, and evaluation, and (2) components external to the training process, such as recruitment and hiring, rewards and incentives, job design, supervision and coaching, co-worker relationships, and business planning. The external components typically have a greater impact on the achievement of training goals than do the internal components. External components are powerful drivers and inhibitors of learning and change.

All the components of the training system must work together effectively to accomplish fully the goals of the organization's larger human performance system. These goals differ somewhat among organizations, but generally the goals of the performance system are to achieve maximum effectiveness and efficiency from human resources, to add value to products and services through effective job performance, and to expand human resource capacity for future organizational success. All the parts of this system must be integrated and coordinated if the goals are to be achieved. For example, a training program that enables supervisors to use a new performance appraisal procedure has little value unless that procedure is supported by appraisal policies and supervisors encourage and reward people for using the new procedure. A lack of fit between even one of these components and the overall system will prevent the achievement of system goals.

This lack of component integration abounds:

The supervisor of a trainee does not think that what the trainee learned in a training session is the right way to do a particular job and discourages any attempts by the trainee to use the new skills.

The procedures taught in training sessions are outdated and inappropriate for the current workplace.

The appropriate audience for the training is not articulated or uniformly agreed upon by managers, and the wrong people are therefore sent to the training sessions.

A department head feels pressured by production demands

and refuses to allow people to attend training sessions that would help them be more productive and advance in the company.

In an attempt to keep an expensive training facility in use, popular new training programs are purchased and advertised even though the training is not a priority need of the company.

Mid-level managers who do not have a background in the training process are given sole responsibility for selecting training programs for their departments.

Top-level management mandates that as part of the new total quality management program all managers and supervisors are empowered to make decisions and correct problems; this is done without changing any of the traditional command and control policies and procedures.

Newly hired employees are taught how to make a part of a machine that the company sells, but the employees are never shown the whole machine, how it works, or how customers use it in their workplace.

Top-level management is making budget decisions about HRD throughout the company, but the only data the managers have to use are the number of people who attended training sessions and their evaluation ratings collected at the end of workshops.

Each of these examples describes system elements that are not in sync with each other. The problems that frustrate training effectiveness are systemic; they are the result of the interaction of system components and not the fault of individuals or one particular component. Employees who cannot attend a needed workshop because their boss is feeling pressure to increase production are being affected by the management incentive and reward subsystem. This element is coming into direct conflict with the career and organizational development subsystem, which is designed to provide individuals with an opportunity to advance and provide skilled personnel to meet strategic goals in the future. Meeting the purposes of one subsystem will impede the success of the other. This is a classic training dilemma. Given the immediate rewards associated with meeting production goals, the training subsystem will be the loser.

Often the system element producing the oppositional forces is not as discrete and identifiable as the problem described above. For example, the elements of the system that cause supervisors to resist empowering their employees are not as obvious but are nonetheless just as strong in hampering the effects of training. Supervisors reluctant to give decision-making power to their subordinates behave this way because their own previous management training taught them command and control, because the incentive and reward program does not reinforce empowerment, because the management style of their boss is command and control, because the process of decision making throughout the company is top-down, because the personnel department does not hire people readily willing to take the risks of empowerment, and because the new hire orientation program does not prepare employees for taking responsibility for their own actions.

The most powerful training force is the organization itself— not the training department. The organization can untrain people much faster than the training department can train them. The task of training leaders who hope to implement highly effective training is to analyze training goals and processes from the perspective of the larger performance system. Then they can identify potential obstacles to training effectiveness and determine the system dynamics that are creating the obstacles. With this information, training leaders can select points of leverage to influence the system, aligning external subsystems with the purposes of training.

One of the points of greatest leverage is the relationship between supervisors and their subordinates. This is a key to teaching and learning within any organization. Supervisors can be sources of knowledge and skills or the brokers for knowledge and skills that their subordinates need to be successful on the job. Supervisors are in the best position to play this role. Professional trainers are too few and too removed from the day-to-day work of most people in the organization to be helpful in this way.

Trainees and supervisors must form a learning partnership, an explicit or implicit agreement that the supervisor will assist the trainee in maximizing the learning process and will support the application of learning on the job. For this to happen, training leaders must give away their skills to supervisors, making them facilitators of learning. Supervisors typically have a tremendous impact on employee learning and the application of learning in any organization, but the impact is haphazard, unstructured, and unfocused. By recognizing the power of this relationship and having a plan, training leaders can leverage these learning partnerships for a much greater impact on the organization.

Training professionals are more familiar with the internal training subsystem components. These internal components are more familiar because they are part of the traditional instructional design and delivery process. The term *instructional system design* (ISD) has become a catchall for these components. For example, a training needs analysis is one of these components. When successful, it provides training leaders with a clear understanding of the organization, group, and individual needs for training. This understanding enables the training leader to design a learning intervention that is likely to produce the desired learning outcome.

Another component of the internal training subsystem is instructional design. This is the set of activities by which knowledge, skills, and attitudes are communicated to the trainee. The elements of the instructional subsystem must fit together well in order for instruction to produce reliable learning outcomes in an efficient manner. This includes elements such as stand-up teaching, self-directed study, various media, and testing and evaluation. If a test that does not measure the instructional objectives of the program is used, immediate dysfunction occurs and learning is threatened.

Ample expertise and guidance on ISD is available in many books and articles. (For example, see Briggs, Gustafson, and Tillman, 1991.) For the purposes of this book, we concentrate on what we have called the external subsystems that affect training. The relationship of these subsystems to successful training is less understood and recognized. Moreover, the most elegant training design or the most exciting presenter cannot help the organization achieve its goals unless training is integrated into the external subsystems. Highly effective training is not only well designed from an ISD perspective, but it is also well integrated with the elements of the organization's broader performance system.

The first step in managing training from a systems perspective is to have a clear understanding of process. Process is dynamic interaction of value-adding activities that operate to produce the desired external goals. Training processes are rarely understood and almost never graphically depicted and communicated to people outside the training department.

The task of HRD professionals is to design processes that will create effective learning and development. These processes should be designed to help employees fit into the picture of what the organization is striving to become. Training process design must be approached with great purpose, much like an architect designs a building to fit the functional use of the occupants as well as the building site, or an engineer designs the body of a car to match the performance specifications of the mechanical system and the needs of the driver. Like the Bauhaus architect or the engineer of a concept car, the form of training should be determined by the function of training.

Example of Systems Thinking
First Ignored and Then Applied

To explain how systems thinking can be applied to designing and managing training, we return to the pharmaceutical company example used in Chapter Six. This is an example of a situation in which inadequate attention was given to systems thinking up front. As a result, the training initially created some major problems before a more systemic approach was used, eventually resulting in a successful program. We first describe the training intervention as it was designed and implemented, pointing out the negative results. Then we analyze the example from the perspective of some of the systems "laws" Peter Senge (1990) discusses in his book on systems thinking. Finally, we show how redesigning the training effort from a more systemic perspective began to produce more effective results.

Systems Thinking Ignored. Communications training was designed for a division of the pharmaceutical company. A communications workshop was developed and delivered to lab workers to teach them assertiveness and probing skills. The focus was on improving their relationships with research scientists.

At the same time, many other divisions in the company were reorganizing. Business competition and lower profits necessitated downsizing. For the first time in decades, employees were being dismissed. Top management had begun to talk about "empowerment" and creating a "flatter organization" as a way of reducing management costs and increasing the productivity of a smaller workforce. A videotape of a popular business guru talking about empowerment had been shown to employees over the lunchtime TV network in the cafeteria.

Several systemic factors were at work to undermine the effects of the training. The training raised employee expectations about being more empowered, regarded, and listened to; made employees more aware of their lack of empowerment; and gave them the skills and the confidence to be more assertive and effective in communicating their needs and expectations.

The lab workers began to use their newly found assertiveness and probing skills to demand more from their managers. Managers were very uncomfortable with this new behavior and interpreted it as rebellious. They responded by exerting more control. Lab workers began spending more time complaining and commiserating with other employees, which caused more lab work delays. Customers, who had become used to better service, noticed the difference and complained to lab management. Lab management responded by canceling all further communications training and became stricter about enforcing work schedules, leaves, and break times. In short, the work environment was considerably worse for lab workers after the training.

The work management system had been based on a less assertive, more docile workforce and a command and control style of management. The change introduced by the training was temporarily successful, but over time its lack of fit with the larger system undermined its effectiveness and exacerbated performance problems.

Analysis. Senge (1990) describes eleven laws of systems. We discuss five of these as they pertain to the situation described above. These laws indicate what needed to be changed in the communications training to ensure its success within the organization.

1. "Today's problems come from yesterday's 'solutions'" (Senge, 1990, p. 57). We must remember that things are the way they are because they got that way. (How profound!) The lab workers were not behaving in empowered ways, but this was not simply out of choice; organization practices and procedures kept them from behaving that way. When they perceived a kind of permission from a communcations course to act empowered, their pent up desire for more authority and responsibility created more problems for management. The first law of systems reminds us to investigate a broad range of causal forces that may not be immediately apparent, including long-standing practices and procedures in the organization. Training professionals should consider these causal forces when designing instructional processes. Either the training must fit the existing system elements, or the elements must be changed to support highly effective training.

2. "The harder you push, the harder the system pushes back" (Senge, 1990, p. 58). When employees were helped to develop the skills to communicate effectively, they began to "push" their bosses for more power and control. But when this pushing created anxiety and suspicion in the bosses, the bosses pushed harder in the opposite direction. And they had the weight of long-standing system practices behind them. When there was a push for more involvement of management in the training, management pushed back harder by canceling the training agreement. Training leaders often experience the effects of this systems law when they are pressured to deliver a training program without regard for real needs and the optimum design. As the trainer and manager "push" with piecemeal training, the system pushes back by resisting involvement.

3. "Behavior grows better before it grows worse" (Senge, 1990, p. 60). As the communications training was delivered, training leaders experienced a brief period of elation and satisfaction as the follow-up data showed that trainees were using their skills on the job. Trainers were especially pleased to see that the use of

better communication was indeed having an impact on efficiency and customer satisfaction. However, this brief departure from the norm of the company's long-standing management practices was soon ended, and the relationship of lab workers to managers was worse than before the project began.

4. "The easy way out usually leads back in" (Senge, 1990, p. 60). The company was tempted by what appeared to be an easy solution to a problem. The solution was particularly attractive because of the sense of urgency driven by cost and revenue concerns. However, trying to change employee behavior at the level of the lab worker without parallel changes in management and other components of the external subsystem was a short-term fix that did not work. The apparent shortcut to success took the effort back to the starting point.

5. "The cure can be worse than the disease" (Senge, 1990, p. 61). The training resulted in a partial solution to the quality problem. As only a partial solution, however, the training created new problems and exacerbated existing problems. Having lab workers communicate more effectively could not be limited simply to their interactions with customers. Before the training, lab workers had been resigned to their lack of influence and power. Even though quality problems existed (the disease), operations were relatively stable. The training tipped the balance of the system, interacting with the lab workers' dormant discontent and the external pressures building on the company. Training (the cure) just served to create more tension and disruptiveness.

Systems Thinking Applied

Following several meetings with senior and mid-level lab managers at the pharmaceutical company, there occurred a more systemic intervention. The focus was still on improving the quality of service to customers (research engineers), but everyone had a commitment to bring about deeper and more lasting change. The redesigned intervention called for the learning event (communications training workshop) to be implemented essentially unchanged: half-day sessions spread out over a twelve-week period, with practice assignments between sessions. The difference was that the new intervention employed a number of activities that better integrated the training into the larger human performance system. Change was required beyond the lab worker and customer relationship. Let's look at some of these activities.

Senior and mid-level managers were taught empowerment strategies and a new role for managers. In essence, this training was intended to provide managers with the will and skill to act as supporters rather than controllers of performance. In the past, managers were promoted because they had the technical skills to solve problems; when things went wrong, they could fix them. This led lab workers to depend on managers and, increasingly, to avoid involvement in and responsibility for production and quality. The new role for managers was to empower lab workers. The design of this intervention called for bimonthly clinics where managers would meet to vent their frustrations, support one another, and report on their successes and failures. This training was coordinated by people working on empowerment in other parts of the company as part of the organization redesign and downsizing program.

Managers received the same training as did the lab workers. Because of this, managers were able to coach and reinforce lab workers' new skills. And middle-level managers were able to use the new skills in working with their bosses who had also received the training.

Lab workers were put in charge of their own scheduling. Working in teams, they took more responsibility for work procedures and control of the workplace. In the lab, the lead analyst's job was redefined so that this person became a team leader who facilitated decision making but had no more power than any other worker.

Lab workers designed and implemented new measurement systems so that they could track their own quality improvements. Teams met to review their measures and made recommendations to management about procedural and policy changes.

A compensation program that based compensation on actual production results as averaged over each month's data was developed. Under this system, teams could earn bonus pay as they and other participating teams achieved higher productivity and quality goals.

Lab workers analyzed their jobs to identify their major customers and internal suppliers. They examined the outcome requirements of both of these groups and were encouraged to communicate directly with their customers and suppliers. Managers agreed to support cross-functional teams formed to help the lab meet customer requirements. This new interaction with customers and suppliers opened new arenas for the application of recently learned communication skills. Such interaction provided leverage for making quality improvements that could be initiated by the lab workers and their teammates.

Obviously, the redesigned intervention took account of many more systemic factors. The new approach also required more time and was considerably slower in developing than the earlier nonsystemic effort. Participants recognized that lasting change would take more time than a quick fix and accepted the fact that all parties to the change effort would need to take risks, be willing to learn from experience, and cooperate with one another. The painful results of the earlier intervention were persuasive; those involved realized that there was much to be gained in the long run from a more system-wide approach.

Process Management: A Tool for Training Systems

The key to the shift to HET lies in managing training as an integrated process that necessarily crosses functional boundaries in the organization. This is quite different from the much more common approach: managing training as an independent program or learning intervention that lies within the scope and purview of a training department. In the pharmaceutical example, the systemic approach involved many nontraining individuals and functions. Training was managed as a cross-functional process.

One of the management tools that helped in the application of the principles and practices of systems thinking to the pharmaceutical company was *process management*. Many leading-edge organizations, such as Eastman Kodak, Wal-Mart, Xerox, and the San Diego Zoo ("Unleash Workers and Cut Costs, 1992), have dramatically increased efficiency and effectiveness by implementing process management strategies. Such management reorganizes the way that work projects are typically designed and conducted. The method focuses on processes that produce external results as opposed to tasks driven by short-term departmental objectives. The essential precepts of process management have important implications for the practice of training.

Vertical Management versus Process Management

Organizations tend to become increasingly bureaucratized as they grow. Giving separate departments responsibility and accountability is a common way for managers to control input and output. Figure 8.1 shows the familiar bureaucratic structure of departments that can be found in most organizations today. The organization is built like a pyramid, with overall power and decision making centralized at the top and specialized functions and decisions directed from the top of each department. This structure can be very useful in achieving a number of important objectives. It helps clarify who is responsible for what, making management easier. It promotes efficient completion of tasks, such as marketing or financial analysis. However, as the organization grows, departments grow and create greater and greater distances between themselves. Eventually, the quality and efficiency of product development or service delivery are affected.

Customer needs often go unmet as a result of department-level efforts to achieve department-level objectives. For example, a shipping department may hold small orders until a sufficient number of orders are accumulated to warrant sending them out in bulk. This appears to be a more cost-effective way of handling orders than sending out each order separately. However, this practice might not meet the customer's need to have an order arrive in a timely manner.

Often, vertically organized companies experience conflict between departments, wasting time and valuable resources attempting to overcome barriers to effectiveness caused by departmental work boundaries. Deming, in a November 1992 speech in Kalamazoo, Michigan, illustrated the effects of work boundaries with the exam-

Figure 8.1. Traditional Bureaucratic Structure.

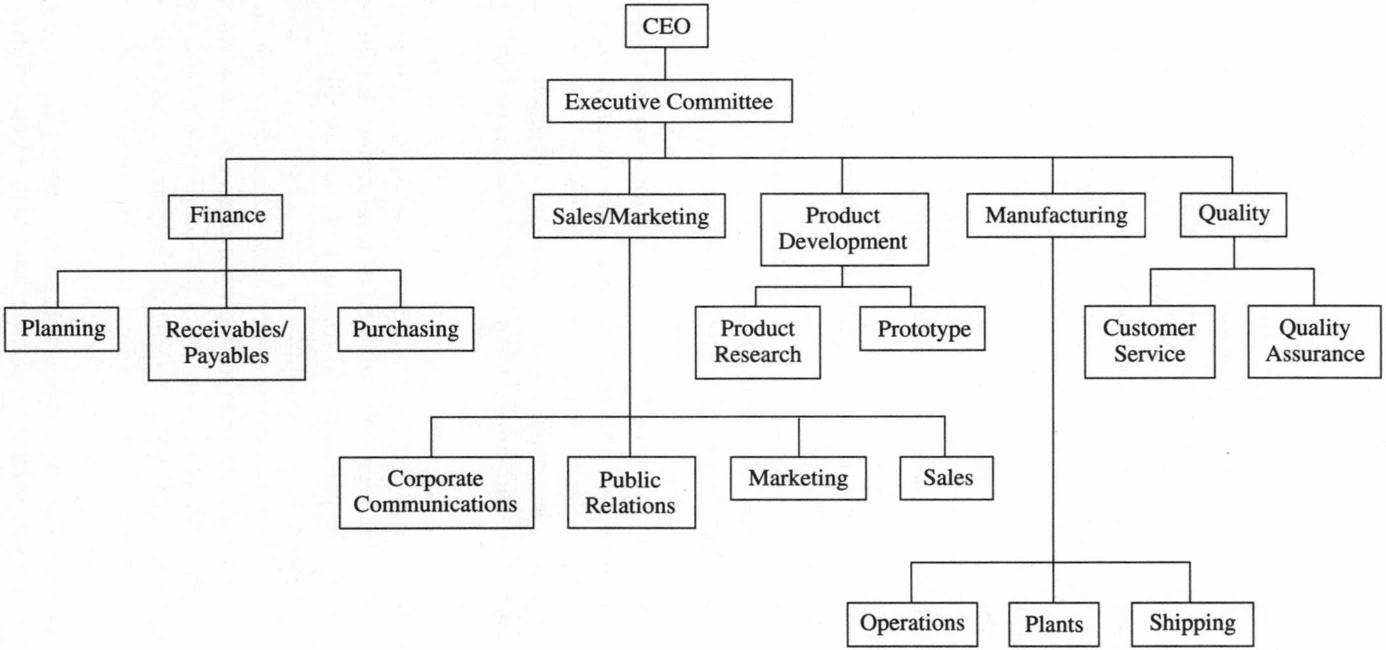

ple of an employee of a large automobile company. While working in the engine department, this employee discovered that an additional part would improve the performance of the fuel injection system. His idea was rejected by senior management because it would have added $30 to the cost of each engine and the engine department's goal was to reduce engine costs. However, the part would have enabled the engine to perform in such a way that the transmission could have been modified. This modification would have allowed the transmission department to reduce the cost of the transmission by $80, thus reducing the overall cost per car by $50. The departments of this company were working independently toward their own goals; they were not working collectively toward the goals of the external customer.

The critical flaw in vertical organization is that no one has control over the key cross-functional processes that produce the goods and services the customer desires. This organizational structure, in effect, pits department goals against organization goals, leading to suboptimization and failure to meet worthy customer goals.

Both horizontal and vertical organizations group tasks into processes. The main difference between these types of organizations is that in the vertical organizations, tasks are grouped by task specialty or similarity. For example, purchasing tasks are centralized in a purchasing department, marketing is handled in a marketing department, and employment issues are addressed in a personnel department.

In the horizontal organizations, tasks are organized by function, such that all tasks that are functionally linked to achieving the same results, regardless of their specialization, are joined in the same process. Management control and responsibility are dedicated to that process. For example, a team charged with improving a company's sales ordering system might include people involved in sales, order taking, marketing, manufacturing, and shipping. All these people have responsibility for completing a process for a customer that starts with the sale of the product and ends when the product has been received by a satisfied customer. The success of this process is measured by the achievement of external goals, such as on-time delivery of the right order. Figure 8.2 depicts a horizontal, or process-oriented, organization. As this figure shows, horizon-

Figure 8.2. Process-Oriented Structure.

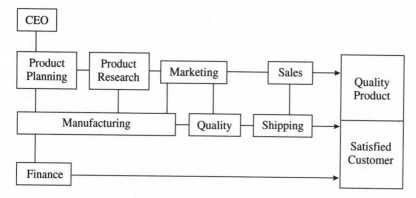

tal sequences of cross-functional tasks are organized to contribute directly to achieving critical external goals.

Process managers and teams work across department boundaries to decrease the time it takes to reach goals and increase the quality of the results, regardless of participants' department affiliations. The Hallmark greeting card company ("Unleash Workers and Cut Costs," 1992) was losing sales because of its department-oriented vertical organization. The company was taking two years to get new card lines onto retailer shelves. Hallmark reorganized its new product development process. Holiday-specific teams were formed. For example, a Valentine's Day team, comprised of artists, creative designers, writers, stock purchasers, printers, and others worked intensively to reduce the time it took to get a new card line to market. The new cards moved directly from function to function, without delay and under constant quality management. This new horizontal structure also saved the company money because it eliminated the delays, rework, and miscommunication caused by the old vertical structure. Most important, the new structure enabled employees to focus on the goal of meeting customer needs rather than the goals of separate departments.

Features of Training Process Management

Process management in a horizontal organization has a number of defining characteristics. These characteristics are listed below, with a brief description of how each is applied to the management of the training process.

• The process is focused on external goals. Managing the critical sequence of tasks that directly contributes to the achievement of important business objectives is the priority. Achieving external goal quality is considered more important than achieving the internal objectives of a department. The purpose of training process management is to add value to the training customers' experience. Meeting customer learning needs should be the focus of the process. This means taking the fastest and the lowest-cost path to the highest-quality training.

• Cross-functional teams ensure the likelihood of process success. All functional areas that contribute to the success of the process must be represented on the team. Team members' ability to share information, work together on common objectives, and be advocates for the process among their peers dictates the level of success. The training process team should include all stakeholders in that process. Typically, the stakeholders are management, the trainees' supervisors, the trainees, the people supervised by the trainees, and external customers. Each of these groups has a stake in the success of training. All of these groups should be represented on the working team that is responsible for making the training successful.

• Individuals are rewarded because of their contribution to the team effort. This requires constant attention to team goals, not to independent tasks that lead only to personal accomplishments. Managing the training process means identifying the specific contribution that each player on the training team must make to the overall goal and then recognizing these contributions as they occur. For example, the coaching that a first-line supervisor provides to trainees working in a factory should be defined as part of the training process and then assessed and rewarded.

• Measures of progress and outcomes are directly and sequentially linked to the important quality goals. These measures facilitate process management by guiding the improvement of the process and indicating when the process has met the customers' needs. The measures of the training process should be linked to trainee performance that is linked to business objectives that are linked to organizational goals that fulfill the mission of the company.

• Processes are the defining organizational units of the company. Hierarchy gives way to goal achievement. This flattens the organizational structure, with lines of authority, communication, and accountability being shortened to facilitate tasks being completed efficiently and effectively. Responsibility for learning interventions is placed where, when, and with whoever can make that intervention successful. The responsibility may be distributed to managers, supervisors, and various support personnel outside of the training functional area (that is, the training department) if this will optimize the process.

• Specific tasks, schedules, and resources are coordinated and kept focused on the goal. Planning and project management tools, such as Pareto charts, Gantt charts, flowcharts, and resource management software, are used for this purpose. The impact map described in Chapter Four is an example of a tool that we use for managing the training process. This tool indicates the link that particular learning and performance objectives have with the value-added goals of the organization. The cross-functional, team-oriented, long-term focus of highly effective training requires a rigorous planning and coordination approach.

• Team members are trained in the knowledge, skills, and attitudes they need to function effectively as a team. The mind-set and behaviors that contribute to good teamwork are not in the repertoire of most employees. Collaborating with someone outside one's own discipline is a foreign notion to many professionals. Even for those who have participated in and contributed to effective teams, ongoing reinforcement of their abilities is still necessary. Professional trainers share this need with their nontraining co-workers. All stakeholders in a particular training process need to develop effective team leadership and membership abilities.

As we have argued in the earlier chapters, the desired end results of training are produced by a process that transcends typical department boundaries. In nearly every business that attends to the training and development of its employees, a separate department (sometimes this is just one designated person) is charged with designing and delivering learning interventions. Yet the overall process, from needs identification to training goal setting and proceeding to transformation of new skills and knowledge into enhanced job performance, spans several arenas of management.

Supervisors of trainees play a pivotal role in the success of this process. Their behavior is a major determinant of whether or not training-acquired knowledge and skills ever get used correctly on the job. Supervisors often determine the attitude that the trainee brings to the training event. Supervisors approve the amount of time and money that someone can use for training. Supervisors provide the time and opportunity for the newly trained employee to use the new knowledge and skills. Supervisors can provide the reinforcement needed to ensure that trainees learn and repeatedly apply the learning to their work.

The paradigm that drives training and development programs today is precisely the productivity conundrum that the horizontal management approach aims to address: no one has control over the entire process that produces the external, value-added goals of training. The primary barrier to effective management of training is the misconception rampant in most organizations that training is the responsibility of training specialists or a formally structured training department. Therefore, the essential task of reform is to change this misconception and in its place install an effective, cross-functional training process management system.

We are not suggesting that this reform is easy to accomplish. Organizational systems, like biological systems, have their own optimal rate of change and growth. Forcing them to move faster than this rate can result in the system compensating by slowing down or even behaving in a self-destructive way.

This is especially true when we are using the training process as a vehicle for bringing about major changes in an organization. Many organizations today want to change their culture or the way they do business, but this does not mean that these organizations will readily and easily embrace change. Many management innovations have been short lived because the target audience was not ready or was not given enough time to implement them. Consider how much training time and money have been invested by some companies in quality circles only to achieve little or no impact on the goals of the organization.

One large electronics firm has decided to change the way it produces new products. The company realizes that if it is going to compete in the world market, it must produce new products more rapidly, at lower cost, and with higher quality. This change requires retraining everyone in the company on innovation, design, and production processes that are quite different from the way the company has been doing business.

Because of its vertical organization, this company has been using a serial process of development for new products. That is, the research and development department comes up with an idea, the engineering design department takes that idea and designs a product on paper, the models department takes the blueprints and creates a model, manufacturing takes the model and builds some prototypes, then the marketing department figures out how to sell the product to a prospective customer, and finally engineering gets back involved to figure out how to adapt the product to the customer's specific requirements and purchasing gets involved to figure out how to get the parts that operations needs to build the redesigned product. This is referred to as the "throw it over the wall" process. When one department is done, it passes the project to the next department with little sense of responsibility for the quality of the final product.

As you can imagine, this is a very time-consuming and highly inefficient process. World-class manufacturing usually means creating a high-quality replacement product every eighteen months. The old way of creating new products cannot even come close to this goal. To meet the world-class customer requirements the company realizes that it will have to use cross-discipline teams. These teams will allow marketing people, design engineers, prototype engineers, purchasing people, and suppliers to be involved with the customer at the very beginning, sharing their expertise and solving design, production, and marketing problems at the earliest point possible in the process.

This change in the company is needed immediately, but the company cannot change immediately. Employees need to accept the new direction. Their natural resistance to change must be overcome. Everyone in the company needs to learn about this new product development process and their role in it. They need to learn how to work in cross-discipline teams and how to use project management and quality control tools designed especially for this process. It has taken two years to just figure out how the company wants to change and what specifically employees need to learn. Another two years will be required to develop and deliver the training for the most critical group of employees. Then there will be several years of maintenance of the culture change before the company can be confident that the new process has been successfully integrated.

If this electronics company had tried to force an overnight change, it would have met considerable resistance that would have sabotaged the effort and threatened the viability of the organization. Faster would have been much slower. Motorola, another electronics company, took nearly ten years, using intensive training at all levels in the corporation, to achieve their goal of six sigma in the quality of all products.

Summary

The essence of managing training with a systems view of learning in the organization is systems thinking. This represents a shift in the way most people think about training. The shift is from departmentalized to interdependent, from program to process, from quick fixes to analytic solutions, from short-term results to long-term results, from costly change to leveraged change, and from blaming the system to owning the system.

Barriers, in the sense of old ways of thinking about performance improvement and organizational behavior, are represented by the separation of work and learning and the compartmentalization of business functions. One tool that can be used to overcome these barriers is process management, which leverages the resources of an organization by integrating people and functions and improving communication. Another tool that can be used for this purpose is the impact-mapping technique described in Chapter Four. Measurement and feedback, essential to applying these tools and to applying systems thinking in general are discussed in Chapter Nine.

9

Using Measurement and Feedback for Continuous Improvement

This chapter focuses on the fourth principle of HET: measure the training process for the purpose of continuous improvement. Highly effective training depends on continuous measurement to keep the process on track toward achieving business goals. We believe that performance improvement systems will not succeed without a continuous process of data collection and feedback.

Given the first three principles of HET, measurement should focus on the linkage of training to business goals, needs of the different customers, and the interaction of components of the organization's system. More specifically, measurement can be used for the following purposes in the HET approach:

- To identify opportunities for training
- To determine customer deficits in needed knowledge, skills, and attitudes
- To enhance the learning process
- To manage critical value-adding events
- To identify training problems and their potential solutions
- To assess the business impact of training
- To provide accountability for the use of resources
- To monitor changes in attitudes and perceptions related to training

This chapter describes how to make ongoing measurement a tool for achieving these purposes and examines the key elements of this measurement process as they relate to each of the four sub-processes of HET. A full explanation of how to apply various measures and the analysis of data is beyond the scope of this book, but many helpful resources are available (see Brinkerhoff, 1987; Goldstein, 1986; May, 1987; Phillips, 1983; Spencer, 1986; Steadham, 1980).

Continuous Measurement

Continuous improvement is a very useful concept that we have taken from total quality management. This notion is that any product or process should be open to regular and frequent measurement for the purpose of reducing errors and defects and increasing quality.

Continuous improvement of training requires continuous measurement of all aspects of the process of helping employees learn and change. Just as effective training programs must have goals, attentive students, a facilitator, instructional materials, and an opportunity to practice new skills, training must also have a means of feedback on the status of process and performance. Measurement that begins early in the process can be used to set goals, improve instruction, and ensure transfer to the workplace. Measurement must occur throughout the learning process if training is to achieve its maximum impact.

Highly effective training uses program evaluation as a tool for continuous improvement. People need feedback of evaluation data to tell them what changes are needed, how best to make those changes, and when those changes have been successfully completed. Measurement is a tool to help training departments achieve and maintain change through quality programs (May, 1987).

Measurement is not only counting the number of something, such as the number of trainees attending a learning event, the number of answers trainees get right on a test, or the number of products sold in the weeks after a sales training session. Measurement also means determining the size and extent of the impact of a training intervention, examining the characteristics of participants, describing in detail the delivery of the training, and documenting any unanticipated outcomes.

However, in practice, measurement is rather limited, and it is usually focused on the learning event, not the training process as a whole. This lack of process and impact measurement can be explained, in part, by time, money, and energy running out by the time training leaders begin to give evaluation serious thought. Under the pressures of their day-to-day work, many training leaders feel that it is quite enough just to deliver a course, workshop, or seminar.

Other explanations for the lack of measurement and evaluation have more to do with mind-set than with resources. One of these explanations for the lack of measurement throughout the training process can be attributed to Kirkpatrick's model of evaluation. For more than thirty years, this model has been a guide for the evaluation of training programs (Kirkpatrick, 1975). The model posits four levels of evaluation that training leaders should observe and suggests that each level of evaluation is successively more difficult and more important to measure. This model has provided a practical framework for conceptualizing and implementing training evaluation. Training leaders nearly always measure the first level, participants' reactions to the event. Typically, they do this by having participants fill out a short questionnaire at the end of the session. Sometimes training leaders measure the second level, knowledge, by testing for information learned during the session. They measure level three, behavior change, and level four, results in the workplace, much less often. While a significant contribution to the HRD field, Kirkpatrick's model has kept the focus on the event, not the process. We must create ways to measure the entire training process and the effects of its various components.

Another explanation for the limited application of evaluation is the use of the instructional system design model for creating instructional programs. This model has been a very useful tool for developers of instructional courses and materials (Briggs, Gustafson, and Tillman, 1991). However, the model is lacking in a systems view of the work environment. By positioning evaluation (both formative and summative) as two of the last steps in the model, ISD implies that measurement is the last activity that an instructional developer needs to think about.

The HRD profession may have inadvertently misled practitioners about the complexity of measuring training. The method depends entirely on the purpose of training in the particular organization. If the purpose of a training department is to conduct well-attended courses, then measurement is quite simple. Count the number of people who attend and compare this number to the number of people who could have attended. A high percentage indicates success, and a low percentage indicates that the program should be changed. However, if the purpose of training is to help the organization achieve its goals, then the measurement process is much more challenging. These goals are not always clear. When we ask, training leaders say that the purpose of their training programs is to teach the information and skills employees need to be successful in their work. But then when we ask these same training leaders what they measure, they mention the number of people who attended, how often the course is requested, and ratings from the end-of-session evaluation forms. The stated goals for the training and the aspects of training that are measured are not congruent.

The entire training picture must be brought into focus; a close-up of the trainee will leave out a background that is critical for understanding impact. Given that training is a process within a system and that the system affects the implementation and outcomes of training, important aspects of the process and the system must be measured, not just the learning event. Measuring the learning event without considering the system in which that event occurs, is like diagnosing an illness by just taking a person's temperature.

An illustration of how risky it is to limit assessment to only one part of the training process is an evaluation of a course for an automobile company's engineers. The course was designed to teach a new quality process improvement technique. The training leaders conducted a follow-up survey of the trainees to determine whether this course had any impact on the engineers' work. According to this survey, only a very small percentage of training participants used the method after the course.

One could conclude that the learning event was not effective. However, by measuring the process as well, the training leaders learned that supervisors did not prepare the trainees for the course, many of the participants did not have an opportunity to use the new technique in their work for months after the course ended, supervisors did not allow trainees the necessary time on their jobs to practice the technique, and although the technique was required, it was not valued throughout the organization. From this combination of measures, the training leaders concluded that the problem was not the learning event but rather factors external to the course.

Measurement should help training leaders determine whether the training goals fit the needs of the trainees and whether the training strategy (for example, classroom instruction, self-instruction, on-the-job training) is the best strategy for the situation. Measurement should help training professionals assess progress toward goals and immediate learning and behavior change and help them examine the extent to which the learning and behavior change endures in the organization and has an impact on business success.

At the beginning of this chapter, we listed several key purposes for measurement. Here we briefly explain each of these purposes in the HET approach.

• *To identify opportunities for training.* This information is used to validate the linkage between projected training outcomes and the business goals and strategic objectives of the organization. Data are collected by the more traditional methods of needs assessment, the performance analysis techniques associated with front-end analysis (see Harless, 1981; Rummler and Brache, 1991) and the methods proposed in Chapter Four for mapping the events and interim results that verify that training is helping to achieve the business goals.

• *To determine customer deficits in needed knowledge, skills, and attitudes.* This information is used to design compatible and effective training strategies. The gap in skills, knowledge, and attitudes between where employees are now and where they need to be is measured. The precision of a measure can vary from the counting of computer data entries to managers' self-reports of their level of confidence in meeting facilitation skills.

• *To enhance the learning process.* Measurement can have a direct impact on the learning process. A truism seems to be that if you measure something it will improve. Trainee learning objectives are derived from measured levels of job performance and competence. Learning progress is facilitated by regular measurement (such as testing) of accumulated skills, knowledge, and attitudes. Measures of competence levels that are achieved can reinforce and motivate trainee learning.

• *To manage critical value-adding events.* As explained in the stories of Jan and Michael, the training process is characterized by a number of critical value-adding events. When these events are managed before, during, and after a learning intervention, they provide leverage for increasing impact. These critical value-adding events must be measured and tracked to ensure their effectiveness and to apply the lessons learned to future training.

• *To identify training problems and their potential solutions.* Because training is part of a larger system, ad hoc teams representing cross-functional responsibilities are often formed to solve the inevitable problems that can prevent successful training. Measures of training progress indicate when these teams are needed. The teams then use these data to solve problems and assess their success.

• *To assess the business impact of training.* The business impact of training interventions is measured so that decisions about needs for additional training can be made. The ultimate goal of training should be to achieve business goals. Therefore, business impact data are used as indicators of the effectiveness of the training process.

• *To provide accountability for the use of resources.* Training, like any other activity in the organization, must be accountable for its use of resources. Measurement data are needed to track and verify resource utilization. This use of measurement assesses impact and indicates value in relation to the time, money, and materials expended.

• *To monitor changes in attitudes and perceptions related to training.* Measurement keeps people focused on the elements of the process that are important. Implementing processes within the new paradigm requires a change in attitudes and perceptions. The approach places unfamiliar demands on both training and non-training personnel. Keeping important parties involved and committed requires considerable coaching, persuading, motivating, and cajoling. Such measurement data and efforts are an essential part of the paradigm.

Type of Measurement Tool

The specific measurement tool to be used is determined by the type of data that is needed. A test of the trainees' knowledge might be appropriate in one situation, while interviews with the supervisors of the trainees might be appropriate in another. We start by defin- ing the questions. (It is not hard to find the answers, it is the ques- tions that are difficult.) This helps us focus measurement on the data that are truly important to us and to making training highly effective. Questions need to be answered in every phase of the train- ing process.

We have found the following questions helpful in improving each HET subprocess:

Formulating Training Goals

What is the need?
How great is this need, problem, or opportunity?
Is it amenable to a training solution?
Is the organization ready for and supportive of a training intervention?

Planning Training Strategy

Would the training intervention be worthwhile?
Would the training be likely to pay off?
Are there criteria for judging whether it paid off or not?
Is the training intervention better than alternative ap- proaches? What will work?
What will work best?
Which design is best under the circumstances?
Can the design be implemented?
What kind of support for the new learning can be expected from immediate supervisors and the organization?
Do the training design and training materials have the qual- ities of good training?
Is the process likely to succeed?

Learning Outcomes

Is the implementation working?
Has the training been implemented as it was designed?

Is the training process on schedule?
What are the problems?
How is the training actually being conducted?
What are trainees' reactions to the training?
What does the training cost?
Did trainees learn what they were supposed to learn?
What did trainees learn?
How do trainees plan to use what they have learned?
What kind of help will they need in using their training on
the job?

Supporting Performance Improvement

Are trainees retaining what they learned?
How are trainees using what they learned?
Has the training affected their behavior on the job?
How well are they using what they have learned?
What aspects of the training are they using and what aspects
are they not using?
What difference does applying the learning and behavior
change make to their jobs?
Is this difference worthwhile?
Was it worth the effort and cost?
Has the need been met, the problem solved?
What else is needed?
What should training do next?

Examples of Measurement

Examples of how measurement has been used in each of the sub-processes of HET illustrate its importance and application. The general intent in each case is to assess linkage of training to business goals, response of training to customer needs, and integration of learning into the total system.

Formulating Training Goals

An office furniture company was planning to consolidate most of its training functions into a new facility near its corporate headquarters. Although the company was already considered excellent in terms of HRD, senior management wanted their training programs to provide a competitive edge in the very competitive office furniture industry. They wanted to maximize current programs and create new ones that would prepare employees for change in the industry. They had three major questions: (1) What does the company do currently to train, educate, and develop all of its employees? (2) How effective are these current programs? and (3) What kinds of training programs will the company need in the future (Gill, 1989)?

Two project advisory committees, made up of two levels of key managers, were formed to guide the activities of the project. These groups decided to conduct an exhaustive inventory of current training in the company by conducting interviews with training managers in all departments. To answer the question about the quality of current training, the customers of training were interviewed in focus groups. These customer groups represented each of the major functions within the company (operations, sales, finance, human resources, research and development, marketing and communications, and administration) and the dealerships who sell the products. Following the group interviews, a survey of a sample of employees (training customers) across the corporation was conducted. Input on future needs came primarily from members of senior management, who were also interviewed.

All the data collected through this project were used to create a strategic plan for human resource development. The key to the development of this plan was having senior management inform the task forces about the business goals of the company and then using this information to make decisions about the future of training. The project provided a measure of current and future needs in terms of the business goals of the corporation.

Planning Training Strategy

An electronics manufacturing company had committed itself to a new product development process in order to compete with other major electronics parts suppliers. The purpose of the new process was to reduce dramatically the time involved in creating new high-quality products and getting them ready for production. Senior management recognized that training was vital to the achievement of this goal.

A team of developers designed the training curriculum that would prepare employees for this new way of doing business. Given the topics (such as project management, teamwork, and product reliability) and given the culture of the organization, the project team designed a curriculum that included self-paced instructional modules, audio and video background material, learning partnerships between employee and supervisor, work group activities on the job, and action planning for using the skills gained from the courses. Because this was a new way of delivering instruction within that organization, the instructional strategy needed to be validated.

As a first step, the strategy was presented to all of the training managers within the company. Their reactions to the strategy were collected systematically and used to make adjustments in the design and in the way the training would be initiated in the organization. Next, a prototype of the instructional materials, including a guide for supervisors of trainees, was presented to three focus groups of customers of the training and three groups of supervisors (also customers of training). These groups were asked to predict how effective each of the specific elements of the curriculum would be. The resulting data were used to make additional adjustments to the program. Finally, still other measurements of customer reactions were conducted during a pilot run of the course within the company. Data from this pilot project was used to make more modifications in the curriculum before installation of the program.

Producing Learning Outcomes

A regional gas utility installed a new home service program. Consumers could purchase service contracts from the company and then call home service representatives whenever there was a problem with their gas-fired system. The current employees had to be given the knowledge, skills, and attitudes that would make them successful in providing this new service. They needed to be prepared for anything, from an inaccessible furnace to an angry consumer.

A curriculum had been designed and was being implemented by experienced instructors, but there was concern that the course was not on target for employees new to field service jobs. The approach was to examine the integrity of the course design. The course was measured against a standard that assumed instruction should include course goals, instructional objectives, performance objectives, relevant examples, opportunities to practice skills, tests of knowledge gained, tests of skill performance, and coherence among all these elements. Course materials were analyzed, and selected course sessions were observed. The findings were presented to the instructors, who discussed the extent to which each course met the standard and what they could do to fill any gaps. Not only did the instructors find out about the quality of their own courses, but they learned more about instructional design, which would help them with future courses.

Supporting Performance Improvement

A university offered training to the supervisors, staff, and volunteers who worked in adult day care centers and senior centers. These centers typically had very few financial resources and very little opportunity for staff development and wanted to improve the professionalism of their workers and increase the quality of their service to clients and client families. Much of the training focused on effective communication between people and on understanding the aging process. The centers were willing to support this training, but only if it provided direct benefits to them and helped them achieve their goals. A series of six monthly workshops was offered to staff members three times over the course of three years.

An evaluation of the long-term impact of the project was then conducted. Three measures were used to assess the impact. One measure was an interview that asked trainees, six months to a year after their last training session, to recount examples of how they had used the information, skills, and attitudes discussed in the workshops, as well as any unintended consequences of the training.

Another measure was an interview of the trainees' supervisors. They were asked to recount incidences in which they observed the trainees applying the content from the workshops. The supervisors were also asked about how the training affected the centers and to what extent each organization supported the application of the new learning to the job.

The third measure was a paper-and-pencil survey of all participants in the workshops over the three years of the project. Trainees responded to questions about how they used the content in their work, how they thought the training could be improved, and what additional performance improvement needs they had. The data from all three measures were consolidated, reported to the center directors, and used to plan future programs.

Value-Adding Measurement Strategies

When it comes to measurement, training leaders tend to become fixated on the measurement tool (usually a survey) and the statistical analysis of data. Sometimes this fixation even paralyzes them. However, useful measurement depends more on deciding what data to collect and for whom than it does on the elegance of the method. In other words, involving stakeholders up front and helping them use the information are more important than which measurement tool is used.

We have found that a number of stakeholder-involving strategies add considerable value to the use of measurement for continuous improvement. These strategies are described below.

Involve Customers in Deciding What to Measure and How to Measure It

Measurement data will have more meaning, and therefore more usefulness, to the customers of training if they have something to say about the measures. One of the most powerful questions one can ask managers is, What do you want to know about this training program? This causes managers, who may have felt disconnected from the training department, to think about training in relation to their needs and goals. They begin to see training as something that could be of significant benefit to them. By asking trainees about what should be measured, the training professional causes them to consider what is important about the process to them, reinforcing their own learning.

Helping managers and others use measurements throughout the training process is not easy. They are not used to being involved in the continuous improvement of HRD programs. Yet without their involvement, it is impossible to make the changes that are necessary for highly effective training. The training leader may need their support for acquiring resources, for recruiting the appropriate trainees, for offering just-in-time training, and for supporting and reinforcing the learning after the training event. Therefore, involvement is key.

Choose the Method of Measurement
Only After Deciding What to Measure

Deciding what to measure before how to measure echoes the architect's principle that form follows function. Perhaps because it appears to be easy to design and use, the paper-and-pencil questionnaire, with five-point (Likert) scales, has become the modus operandi of training leaders. No matter what the purpose of the measurement, most training leaders use a questionnaire to gather the data. However, the questionnaire is only one method among many that can be used to measure various aspects of the training process. Moreover, considerable skill and art are required in designing a questionnaire that will produce valid, reliable, credible, and useful data.

Other measures include individual interviews, group (for example, focus group) interviews, personal observation (or photography or videotape), trainee logs or journals, expert testimony, computer-aided surveys, case studies, audits to verify program content, criterion-referenced standardized tests, telephone-aided audience response system, and examination of the organization's archival data. (See Steadham, 1980, for additional thoughts about these methods.) Each of these measures is only appropriate if it will elicit data that are useful to the trainer and the training customers in a particular situation.

If the question concerns the demographic characteristics of trainees, then a questionnaire might be useful (provided this data cannot be culled more easily from existing records). If the question is how trainees applied their new knowledge and skills to their jobs, interviews of the trainees and their supervisors sometime after the learning event are appropriate. If the question is about the relation-ship of the timing of the training event to changes in business indicators, archival data that track business performance might pro-vide the answer. Useful, credible information is a result of selecting a measurement method that produces the kind of data needed to answer the question.

Report Data That Are Credible to the Customer

Different customers of training may find certain kinds of data more credible than other kinds. Senior HR managers may want to see "the numbers": how many people are participating in how much training at what cost. Direct supervisors may just want a written report that compares what the trainee is learning to what he or she will need on the job. Some managers have told us that it is not nec-essary to conduct a training needs assessment because they can tell us what the employees need. Other managers have told us that nothing short of a comprehensive, standardized, three-hour written and performance examination will convince them of employees' training needs. More than one company has purchased a million-dollar training program because an executive attended a session and thought the program would be great for his or her employees. En-gineers who will not change a process or a product without mounds of statistical data will authorize or change a training program be-cause of testimonials and hearsay.

Training leaders have a responsibility to inform training customers about the effective and responsible use of measurement methods and data. Because the customers may not be trainers them-selves, they may not know what kind of data will answer their questions. This needs to be explained.

Report Findings so the Customer Can Hear Them

The vehicle used to convey information to people influences how and to what extent they hear it. The customer for the data dictates the manner in which it is best to convey them. Training leaders tend to rely on written reports, sometimes lengthy ones. These have a place but are not always the best format for getting the customer's attention. Engineers may prefer charts and graphs, other training leaders may prefer brief written reports, and sales and marketing managers may prefer creative uses of media with an oral presentation. Collecting the right information throughout the training process is not enough. It must be conveyed to the user in a manner that will make him or her take notice, think about it, and act on its meaning. Otherwise, measurement will fail to support the continuous improvement process.

Measure the Process as Well as the Outcome

As we have argued throughout this book, training is a process affected by an organizational system. Training is not merely a learning event. To measure only the outcomes of that learning event is an "inspection" approach and does not prevent problems or ensure the quality of the training. In highly effective training, measurement must start at the beginning and continue throughout the process.

The process within the learning event also deserves attention. Measuring the needs of the participants, their reactions to initial components of the event, their performance on subtasks, the organization's response to the training activities, and the usefulness of various instructional strategies can provide data to improve the learning process. The data should be collected before the attention of the participants and the credibility of the program have been irretrievably lost.

Provide Just-in-Time and Just-Enough Information

Data should be collected when it is available but reported to users as it is needed. Such timing maximizes the impact of the data. Managers in an operations department may need information just prior to preparing their budget for the next fiscal year. Training leaders may need information while revising the design of a course. Trainees may need information while they are using their new skills on the job.

Collecting data that no one will use wastes valuable time and money. The findings of an end-of-session evaluation form might be interesting to the training leader, but why use the form if no one else is going to see the data? An evaluation-type form used early in a learning event often produces similar data, which the training leader can then use immediately to modify the program for the current trainees.

Measure to Improve the Process, Not to Blame or Punish

Data should be collected and reported only if they will be used positively to improve the training program, increase its impact, or increase its visibility. If the customers of training begin to believe that measurement leads to negative consequences for themselves and others, they will not participate fully in the measurement tasks and will not do what is necessary to achieve highly effective training.

This is not easy. Most training leaders tend to be defensive about their instructional ability, even when they are teaching something for the first time or when no one expects them to know how to teach a particular skill. They tend not to listen for what they can learn and use; rather, they only hear a message that is critical of them. Even data as seemingly nonthreatening as measures of training needs may strike some training leaders as critical of the current training effort. This is all the more reason to involve training leaders and the customers of training in the design of the measures. Such involvement will give them a sense of control and influence over the kinds of data being collected and a greater understanding of the usefulness of the data. Then they will be more likely to listen to the data's message when it is reported.

Summary

Measurement of training is useful in linking training to business goals, responding to the needs of training's different customers, and integrating training within the organization's system. In the old approach to training, measurement tends to be limited to assessing immediate trainee reactions to learning events. In the new approach, measurement is crucial to the continuous improvement of the quality of training. HET expands the function of measurement to the entire training process. This approach uses measurement to achieve a number of purposes, all contributing to the quality of training from the perspective of its various customers.

The type of measurement tool to be used is determined by the nature of the data needed to answer the questions posed by the various stakeholders. These questions and the strategies to answer the questions are somewhat different during each of the four sub-processes of HET. The effectiveness of any of these measurement tools and strategies is dependent on the level of involvement of key stakeholders. They should be involved in deciding why, what, how, and when to measure aspects of the training process.

With this chapter we complete our explanation of the four principles of HET. We recognize that the transition from the old program-driven paradigm to the emerging system-focused paradigm that HET represents will require time and nurturing on the part of training leaders. To assist in this process, Chapter Ten suggests ways to help organizations make the shift and includes a checklist for training leaders to use to take stock of how close their organizations are to the HET approach and all the concepts discussed in this book.

10

Making the
Paradigm Shift

We recognize that many readers work in environments characterized by traditional program-driven training. In these settings, strategies for performance improvement must be transitional. These readers must straddle the line between program-driven and system-driven training and try to bring their organizations along to the new paradigm. Therefore, this chapter describes strategies that we have used to bring about the change and provides a checklist that should help readers conduct an HET audit of their organizations. The checklist also serves as a review of the training subprocesses, HET principles, and HET actions described throughout the book.

Strategies

The following strategies are formulated to facilitate a transition to highly effective training within very traditional settings, that is, settings where bureaucratic structures are deeply embedded and have profoundly shaped training attitudes and expectations. While we recommend the use of all the strategies, singly or in combination, readers should be mindful of the fact that change is likely to be slow. For this change to occur, readers must be continuously responsive to unique contextual factors and be ready to modify approaches and restart efforts when resistance threatens success.

General Strategies

We recommend that readers begin with the following overarching strategies.

Start Small. A big visible project may attract too much attention and, consequently, unacceptable levels of threat and resistance.

Aim for Success. Choose a lower-priority project with a high chance of success. An unsuccessful project at the outset will create negative attitudes toward HET and make further inroads more difficult later on.

Pick a Project That Matters. Although choosing a project that matters sounds like a contradiction of the preceding strategy, this strategy reminds you that you must try to make a difference. Find the delicate balance between a relatively low-priority training goal and one that is important to the organization. Go for strategic linkage.

Demonstrate First and Sell Later. Rather than try to seek converts by talking about what highly effective training would look like, just do it. Then use the results to explain what you have done.

Seek a Champion. Find a manager who is strongly motivated to improve performance and who is willing to try a different approach. Be sure this is someone with whom you can work effectively. Ask this person to head the stakeholder committee.

Do Not Aim for Fame. HET requires a servant mentality, not a messianic urge. If you are driven to prove the new approach, you are likely to fail. If you are driven to do something of value for your business partner, you are likely to succeed.

Make It a Team. HET on any scale, even the smallest demonstration project, can only be implemented successfully with cross-functional support and involvement. You will need to form and nurture the team throughout the training process.

Specific Strategies

With the foregoing strategies in mind, we recommend the following more specific strategies for implementing highly effective training.

Tie an HET Project to a New Business Initiative or Innovation. A new initiative, such as introducing a new product line, a new operating system, or a reorganization of a department, always involves one or more individuals who have championed the innovation. They are committed to seeing it work. Usually, they are eager to find help, and a training leader who comes forward with an interest in the innovation and a willingness to assist is welcomed. Further, the new initiative represents a break with the past, and there is often a spirit of openness to change. This opens the door to a fresh look at how training can serve the new business initiative. Almost all new initiatives pose concomitant training needs in that new skills, knowledge, and ways of thinking are involved. For these reasons, the training leader seeking an opportunity to try new training approaches is likely to find a natural playing field with new business initiatives and innovations.

A large furniture manufacturing company was considering building a corporate training facility in which to house the entire training department. All the training managers, resources, and courses that were being housed in three different buildings would be consolidated in one state-of-the-art facility. A vice president was champion of this plan, and he was committed to the construction of a building that would meet the needs of the company at the time and for many years to come. This created an opportunity to evaluate the current training across the company and to plan strategically for the future. The vice president became a supporter of the strategic value of training and new ways to organize for maximum effectiveness. He was instrumental in gaining support from most of management. Even though the company had been conducting high-quality training programs that used the latest technology, the planning for a new facility opened the door for rethinking the role and value of training (Gill, 1989).

Link Training Leaders to One or More Business Partners. HET, as we have explained, is characterized by linkage to business goals and a customer service mentality. To establish these conditions, a partnership needs to be forged between training staff and managers. In this relationship, the training partner is committed to understanding and serving the needs of the business partner, while the business partner is committed to supporting and participating in the training process.

In one federal agency, two line department managers were faced with a combination of staff reductions and an increased demand for service. They were desperate for assistance and also happened to be very supportive of the training department. A meeting was set up between the training manager and the potential business partners, and they soon struck a deal to work together. The first step was to identify in each line manager's department a specific, important, and relatively short-term (eight to twelve months) business performance objective. One objective they chose was to reduce time in delivery of service by 25 percent while maintaining current quality standards. The training partner then collected data and continued to confer with the line manager until a few very specific training needs and objectives were identified. The training partner arranged for delivery of a highly targeted learning event and supporting job aids. The business partner provided managerial support and encouraged employees to attend the training sessions and use their new skills on the job. When the project ended and there had been a significant impact on service delivery time, the training partner had a strong ally in the line manager and a demonstrated success to market the approach to other departments.

Use Evaluation of Existing Programs to Discover Needs and Opportunities for HET. Even in the most traditional program-driven training organizations, at least some training activities are likely to fit the HET model. Performance improvement activities occur along a broad continuum of effectiveness. Given this premise, a training leader can use evaluation procedures to investigate an existing performance improvement effort to identify areas of high impact or practices associated with highly effective training. Then the training leader can use the information to influence managers and build support for increased involvement by all stakeholders.

A large government agency had invested considerable sums in providing two-week technical information seminars. These sessions were intended to upgrade the professional knowledge of senior field project leaders so that they would be familiar with the latest developments and trends in their disciplines. The information was critically needed by project leaders because the business strategy of this agency was to provide up-to-date advice to foreign governments and development institutions. However, the seminars were under scrutiny because they were expensive. Moreover, informal feedback from participants indicated that not everyone benefitted to the extent desired.

A formal evaluation of the technical seminars was conducted. A sample of trainees were interviewed, and portfolios of evidence of the nature of the impact were put together. The study showed that for about 15 percent of the participants, the training had high impact; they made considerable use of what they had acquired in the seminars. For another 15 percent, the seminars had very low impact. The remaining 70 percent experienced moderate impact. An examination of the conditions surrounding participant selection and attendance showed a clear trend toward just-in-time delivery of training for those in the high impact group and exceptionally ill-timed delivery for those in the low-impact group. However, a large portion of the content was not even pertinent to the needs of the high-impact group. Because of the high cost and infrequency of the seminars, the developers were loading as much content as they could into them in the hope that everyone would find at least something of value. The analysis of factors leading to impact and lack of impact resulted in recommendations that seminars be more frequent, include less content, be geographically closer to trainees, and be targeted more closely at their needs. The design that followed now provides training closer to the time that participants need it and also costs less. Training customers now achieve more impact at less cost and with greater satisfaction.

Use Pioneers to Demonstrate Effectiveness of Training. In the "pioneer" approach, a small group of high-need trainees are recruited to demonstrate the impact of a new performance improvement effort. They are asked to make a special effort to use new skills and knowledge in their work. Training leaders give them special assistance and ask them to keep detailed records of their experiences. These experiences are used to improve the training, integrate the training process into the organization system, and market the training more widely.

A popular, three-day workshop on systematic decision making at one large corporation was shown to have had marginal impact. Only about 20 percent of the trainees reported using what they had learned in the workshop on the job. However, given their jobs and business needs, 80 to 90 percent of the trainees should have been applying their learning. The low transfer rate was due to a complex set of on-the-job impediments.

To try to understand how to better link the training to business goals and make it more customer focused, the training leaders decided to use the pioneer strategy. Six people from a training class of fifty volunteered for the role of pioneer. They were oriented to a performance analysis framework to help them identify and understand the typical obstacles to the application of training to the workplace. Support was provided through meetings with their supervisors and special job aids. The six participants kept detailed logs of their experiences in trying to use the training and took part in regular interviews so that the training leaders could distill key factors from the pioneers' experiences on the job. From the logs and interviews, the training leaders developed a set of guidelines and recommended practices that other trainees and their supervisors could use to achieve maximum impact from the training. The pioneers were especially successful in using their new learning, and several achieved dramatic results in their work. These results were documented and used to illustrate the potential payoff of the training and to build enthusiasm among all managers.

Build Business Linkage Project by Project. The permanent linkage of training to business strategy can be ensured only through an organizational infrastructure that provides a continuing communication channel between training leadership and senior management. Even the smallest performance improvement project can contribute to building this infrastructure.

A large bank was seeking greater sales performance from the retail branches in one of its districts. A steering committee composed of the vice president for district operations, the district sales and marketing director, and three district branch managers was formed. The committee provided occasional oversight to a training project designed to improve sales performance at the branches. The committee, in essence, was one element of the organizational infrastructure needed to support the training process. Two major outcomes occurred because of this committee: (1) performance objectives established for the training project were clearly and directly linked to business strategy at the district level; and (2) the project was given the stature and credibility it needed to solicit involvement and commitment from other branch personnel essential to the success of the training effort. This was a case where a linkage infrastructure was created by keeping it temporary, low level, and specifically targeted at the needs and goals of a single, small, highly effective training project.

The HET Checklist

Assessing where an organization stands in relation to the new paradigm for training is the first step in applying the concepts and strategies described in this book. To help in this assessment we have developed the checklist presented in Exhibit 10.1. The checklist is, in effect, a summary of the book's main points.

The checklist is based on the four principles of highly effective training and the four subprocesses of the total training process. Although this list is an itemization of the elements that we believe must exist before the impact of training can be optimized, we do not claim that it is exhaustive. The emerging paradigm for performance system improvement that we have been describing is not sufficiently coherent to make us confident that we have identified all the elements. Users may find a need to add and subtract items because of their particular training situations.

The checklist is meant to be a guide to a single, interconnected training process. For example, the tool could be used to examine an effort to increase retail market share through the training of sales representatives and district managers in how to use a strategic marketing approach. One major use of the checklist is to guide training development proactively by ensuring that each item is addressed in the design of the training process. Another major use is to retroactively assess the strengths and weaknesses of a particular training process that has already been used in an organization.

Exhibit 10.1. The HET Checklist.

Formulating Training Goals

Linkage Principle
____ Business goals and strategic objectives have been identified.
____ Business strategies are consistent with and important to business goals.
____ Business goals for training are clearly defined and measurable.
____ Impact map has been developed so that the interrelationship of knowledge and skills, job behaviors, job success indicators, business objectives, and strategic goals is evident.
____ There are no critical gaps in the paths on the map (elements will lead to achievement of business goals).

Customer Focus Principle
____ Training goals are based on an analysis of customer needs.
____ Each trainee's learning objectives are consistent with business goals and strategies.
____ All internal and external customers for training have been identified.
____ Customers have been given an opportunity to validate the training goals.
____ Impact map has been discussed and verified with all key stakeholders.

Systems Perspective Principle
____ Learning is valued as part of the culture of the organization.
____ Training goals fit within the organizational system.
____ Pursuing the training goals will not interfere with progress toward other business goals.
____ Effects on the organization of achieving training goals are understood.
____ Effects of the interaction of the elements of the impact map are understood.
____ Effects of the interaction of rewards and incentives, business processes, job design, job tools, technology, and equipment, supervision, and performance assessment on training are understood.

Measurement Principle
____ Training goals are based on credible and accurate data.
____ Learning objectives are based on measures of skill and knowledge levels of trainees.
____ Job performance objectives are based on measures of performance levels of trainees.
____ Achievement of training goals is measurable.
____ Each point on the impact map is measurable.
____ Procedures for assessing progress toward achievement of training goals have been defined.

Exhibit 10.1. The HET Checklist, Cont'd.

_____ Procedures for measuring goal achievement are planned.
_____ Specific criteria for measurement are followed; that is, measurement is ethical and not a threat to human rights or legal constraints, practical, likely to produce accurate data, certain to make use of available data where possible, and likely to produce credible data.

Planning Training Strategy

Linkage Principle
_____ Training design includes opportunities for trainees to question and clarify linkage to business goals.
_____ Training design includes opportunities for trainees to specify their own learning objectives and job performance objectives.
_____ Design of prelearning, learning event, and postlearning activities are optimally integrated with key business processes.
_____ Training activities are consistent with business values and strategies.
_____ Design calls for those with the greatest need and most leverage to achieve business goals to receive training first.
_____ Design is an iterative process of delivery, feedback, and redesign for timely learning and change relative to changing business goals.

Customer Focus Principle
_____ Training customers have had an opportunity to review and react to the training design.
_____ Developers have incorporated customer needs and interests into the design.
_____ Design includes activities that will keep customers informed of trainee progress.
_____ Design includes activities that solicit customers' opinions for changing the design as training progresses.
_____ Design includes specific value-adding activities for each of the several training customers.

Systems Perspective Principle
_____ Priority is for team and large group learning rather than individual learning.
_____ Developers have considered systemic factors that will facilitate the achievement of training goals.
_____ A comprehensive plan has been developed for supporting the training process before, during, and after learning events.
_____ Management control over each learning event and process has been identified and secured.
_____ Design includes cross-functional communication plans to provide feedback to all participants in the training process.

Exhibit 10.1. The HET Checklist, Cont'd.

_____ Design includes activities to manage critical value-adding events before, during, and after learning.

_____ Design includes opportunities for trainees to practice key skills and receive feedback on performance.

_____ Design involves supervisors, peers, and subordinates in helping trainees learn and apply new knowledge and skills.

_____ Supervisors and other leaders have agreed to support learning and encourage the application of new learning.

_____ Learning objectives include awareness of the systemic factors that are likely to hinder and facilitate effective performance.

_____ Performance support tools, such as job aids, and procedures are in place and have been integrated into the overall plan.

Measurement Principle

_____ Design is consistent with the qualities of effective instruction and adult learning.

_____ Design includes procedures for measuring key progress and impact indicators.

_____ Trainees know how to assess their own learning and transfer of that learning.

_____ Measurement activities to assess the design from the viewpoint of the four principles are in place.

_____ Procedures for using data to improve the design are in place.

Producing Learning Outcomes

Linkage Principle

_____ Prelearning materials explain the relationship of training to achieving the business goals of the organization.

_____ Learning event facilitators raise issues and respond to questions concerning the relationship of that event to business needs and goals.

_____ Learning event content, exercises, and examples emphasize business needs and linkage.

_____ Trainees demonstrate an accurate awareness of business needs, strategies, and goals.

_____ Trainees receive just-in-time and just-enough training to maximize leverage of performance.

_____ Trainees receive learning interventions and assistance at precisely the times when the most value will be achieved for the business.

_____ Trainees are off the job the minimum time possible.

Customer Focus Principle

_____ Modifications are made to the training process if warranted by input from customers.

_____ Learning content, exercises, and examples emphasize customer service.

Exhibit 10.1. The HET Checklist, Cont'd.

_____ Trainees identify and understand the needs of their customers.
_____ Learning interventions are scheduled to optimize meeting the individual learning needs of trainees.
_____ Learning interventions are scheduled to minimize disruptions to trainee work responsibilities.
_____ Trainees have the opportunity to modify the training schedule when job or personal priorities impinge on the process.
_____ Trainees have ready access to individuals, materials, and other resources when they have questions and concerns.
_____ No trainees are exposed to unsafe or unethical practices or otherwise placed in situations that might embarrass or offend them.
_____ Learning events and other training activities take place in venues that are convenient, appropriate, comfortable, and pleasant.

Systems Perspective Principle
_____ Trainees understand the systemic factors that bear on effective performance.
_____ Trainees receive continuous support and encouragement for learning, practice, and improved work performance.
_____ Trainees receive guided application of learning with job aids and other performance support tools.
_____ Trainees have frequent opportunities to identify, clarify, and discuss factors that bear on their learning and performance.
_____ Learning interventions are integrated with work processes.
_____ As training constraints and opportunities arise within the workplace, learning interventions are modified accordingly.
_____ Learning interventions have been partitioned into the smallest feasible units.

Measurement Principle
_____ Interaction of training with other operations is assessed.
_____ Trainees receive frequent and accurate feedback on their learning progress.
_____ Learning is assessed at all key points in the training process.
_____ Feedback to customers is as rapid as possible to enable timely learning.
_____ Data about individual learning are safeguarded to protect the rights of individuals.
_____ Measurement instruments and procedures used to assess learning are reliable, accurate, practical, and credible.

Supporting Performance Improvement

Linkage Principle
_____ Impact on important business indicators is regularly tracked.
_____ Impact on important business indicators is reported to key stakeholders.

Exhibit 10.1. The HET Checklist, Cont'd.

_____ Learning is reinforced through repeated interventions.

_____ Application of learning to business needs is supported by supervisors and other leaders in the organization.

_____ Any mismatches between learning interventions and business needs are identified and resolved quickly.

Customer Focus Principle

_____ Training customers with key roles in the value-adding process are constructively involved.

_____ Training customers with key roles in the value-adding process are kept informed of progress, emerging issues, successes, and problems.

_____ Revisions are made in follow-up and reinforcement procedures as a result of changing customer needs.

_____ Customers are assisted in applying the training to their needs.

Systems Perspective Principle

_____ Organizational structure and processes ensure and support the transfer of learning to the production of products or services.

_____ Supervisors of learners provide effective performance support interventions, such as coaching, recognition, and rewards.

_____ Systemic factors that affect transfer of learning to the workplace are managed by the key stakeholders.

_____ Cross-functional communication and collaboration are encouraged during and after the learning event.

_____ Interaction of trainee performance with organizational behavior is examined.

Measurement Principle

_____ Transfer of knowledge and skills to the workplace is monitored.

_____ Measurement instruments and procedures used to assess the transfer of learning are reliable, accurate, practical, and credible.

_____ Impediments to the application of learning are assessed, analyzed, and reported to key decision makers.

_____ Supervisor support for trainee's application of learning to the workplace is monitored.

_____ Reports about the application of learning are provided to key stakeholders.

_____ Trainee performance improvement indicators are regularly measured and reported.

_____ Business performance indicators are regularly measured and reported.

_____ Critical value-adding events are measured, analyzed, and reported to training decision makers.

_____ Measurement and report cycles are short and timely.

_____ Reporting process protects the individual rights of trainees and other stakeholders.

References

Albrecht, K., and Zemke, R. *Service America!* Homewood, Ill.: Dow Jones-Irwin, 1985.

Baldwin, T. T., and Ford, S. K. "Transfer of Training: A Review and Directions for Future Research." *Personnel Psychology,* 1988, *43,* 63–105.

Bowles, J., and Hammond, J. *Beyond Quality.* New York: Putnam, 1991.

Briggs, L. J., Gustafson, K. L., and Tillman, M. H. *Instructional Design: Principles and Applications.* Englewood Cliffs, N.J.: Educational Technology Publications, 1991.

Brinkerhoff, R. O. *Achieving Results from Training.* San Francisco: Jossey-Bass, 1987.

Brinkerhoff, R. O. (ed.). *Evaluating Training Programs in Business and Industry.* New Directions for Program Evaluation, no. 44. San Francisco: Jossey-Bass, 1989.

Brinkerhoff, R. O., and Dressler, D. L. Practical Productivity Measurement: A Guide for Managers and Researchers. Beverly Hills, Calif.: Sage, 1988.

Brinkerhoff, R. O. and Gill, S. J. "Managing the Total Quality of Training." *Human Resource Development Quarterly,* 1992, *3*(2), 121–131.

Broad, M., and Newstrom, J. *Transfer of Training.* Reading, Mass.: Addison-Wesley, 1992.

Carnevale, A. P. *America and the New Economy.* Alexandria, VA: American Society for Training and Development, 1990.

Carnevale, A. P., and others. *Training for a Changing Workforce.* Alexandria, Va.: American Society for Training and Development, 1992.

Churchman, C. W. *The Systems Approach.* New York: Dell, 1968.

Davidow, W. *Total Customer Service: The Ultimate Weapon.* New York, HarperCollins, 1989.

Deming, W. E. *Out of the Crisis.* Cambridge, Mass: Massachusetts Institute of Technology, 1986.

Drucker, P. F. *Managing for the Future.* New York: Dutton, 1992.

Gagne, R. M., and Briggs, L. J. *Principles of Instructional Design.* Troy, Mo.: Holt, Rinehart & Winston, 1979.

Gery, G. J. *Electronic Performance Support Systems.* Boston: Weingarten Publications, 1991.

Gill, S. J. "Using Evaluation to Build Commitment to Training." In R. O. Brinkerhoff (ed.), *Evaluating Training Programs in Business and Industry.* San Francisco: Jossey-Bass, 1989.

Goldstein, I. L. *Training in Organizations: Needs Assessment, Development, and Evaluation.* Pacific Grove, Calif.: Brooks/Cole, 1986.

Harless, J. "Front-End Analysis by Trainers." In *The Best of Training: Interviews and Profiles.* Minneapolis: Lakewood, 1981.

Kimmerling, G. "Gathering Best Practices." *Training & Development,* 1993, *47*(9), 29–36.

Kirkpatrick, D. L. *Evaluating Training Programs.* Alexandria, Va.: American Society for Training and Development, 1975.

Mager, R. F. *Preparing Instructional Objectives.* (Rev. 2nd. ed.) Belmont, Calif.: Lake, 1984a.

Mager, R. F. *Analyzing Performance Problems.* (2nd ed.) Belmont, Calif.: Lake, 1984b.

May, L. S. "Applying Quality Management Concepts and Techniques to Training Evaluation." In L. S. May, C. A. Moore, and S. J. Zammit (eds.), *Evaluating Business and Industry Training.* Boston: Kluwer Academic Publishers, 1987.

Nadler, L., and Nadler, Z. *Developing Human Resources.* San Francisco: Jossey-Bass, 1989.

Peters, T. *Liberation Management.* New York: Knopf, 1992.

Phillips, J. J. *Handbook of Training Evaluation and Measurement Methods.* Houston: Gulf, 1983.

Richey, H. G. *The Theoretical and Conceptual Bases of Instructional Design.* New York: Nichols, 1986.

Robinson, D. G., and Robinson, J. C. *Training for Impact.* San Francisco: Jossey-Bass, 1989.

Rummler, G. A., and Brache, A. P. "Managing the White Space." *Training.* Jan. 1991, 55–70.

Senge, P. M. *The Fifth Discipline.* New York: Doubleday/Currency, 1990.

Spencer, L. M. *Calculating Human Resource Costs and Benefits.* New York: Wiley, 1986.

Steadham, S. V. "Learning to Select a Needs Assessment Strategy." *Training & Development Journal,* 1980, *30,* 56–61.

Tannenbaum, S., and Yukl, G. "Training and Development in Work Organizations." *Annual Review of Psychology,* 1992, *43,* 399–441.

"The Job Drought," *Fortune,* 1992, *126*(4), 62–74.

"Unleash Workers and Cut Costs," Fortune, 1992, *125*(10), 88.

Index